Red Line 4

Grammatiktraining aktiv

Herausgeber: Dr. Frank Haß

Ernst Klett Verlag
Stuttgart • Leipzig

Liebe Schülerinnen und Schüler,

was für Regionen gibt es in den USA und wie ist dort das Schulleben?
Um das herauszufinden, brauchst du nicht nur den geeigneten Wortschatz, sondern auch Grammatikkenntnisse.

Alle Grammatikthemen, die in *Red Line 4* vorkommen, werden in *Grammatiktraining aktiv* noch einmal geübt. Besonders hilfreich sind diese grammatischen Übungen, wenn du z. B. vor einer Klassenarbeit ein bestimmtes Grammatikthema noch einmal gezielt üben willst. Anhand des eingelegten Lösungsheftes kannst du selbstständig nachsehen, was du alles richtig gemacht hast.

In *Grammatiktraining aktiv* findest du dich leicht zurecht, da es genauso aufgebaut ist wie dein Schulbuch. Mithilfe des Inhaltsverzeichnisses kannst du dir einen Überblick verschaffen. Am Anfang eines Grammatikthemas steht die Regel. Daran schließen sich Übungen an, die gezielt diese Regel trainieren.
Auf den Seiten *Grammar mix* am Ende jeder Unit werden verschiedene Grammatikthemen der Unit zusammen geübt. So kannst du deine Kenntnisse abschließend überprüfen.

Das Symbol ● kennst du bereits aus Schülerbuch und Workbook. Diese Übungen sind etwas kniffeliger, aber natürlich sind alle eingeladen, sie trotzdem zu lösen.
Auch in *Grammatiktraining aktiv* findest du Übungen, die du mit einem Partner/einer Partnerin bearbeiten kannst.

Nun wünschen wir dir viel Spaß mit *Grammatiktraining aktiv* und viel Erfolg beim Englischlernen!

Dein *Red Line* Team

Inhalt

G1 R: Die einfache Vergangenheit

Revision: The simple past

Um über Dinge zu sprechen, die in der Vergangenheit passiert und vorbei sind, verwendest du die einfache Vergangenheit (**simple past**).

Signalwörter	
yesterday	gestern
last year	letztes Jahr
a week ago	vor einer Woche
in 2015	(im Jahr) 2015

Das **simple past** bildest du so:
Hänge die Endung **-ed** an das Verb.
Achte auf unregelmäßige Verben, z. B. have → **had**; do → **did**; get → **got**; build → **built**; go → **went** etc.

Eine Liste der unregelmäßigen Verben findest du ab Seite 79.

They **started** roadwork last Monday.	Sie begannen am letzten Montag mit Straßenarbeiten.
Two years ago they **had** a lot of snow in New York.	Vor zwei Jahren hatten sie in New York viel Schnee.

Um zu sagen, was in der Vergangenheit nicht passiert ist, setzt du **didn't** (= did not) vor das Verb.

David **didn't get** into the city.	David kam nicht in die Stadt.

Und so kannst du im **simple past** Fragen stellen:

Did you **have** a good time in New York?	Yes, I **did**.	No, I **didn't**.
When **did** your friend **visit** Manhattan?	Last weekend.	

Aussagen und Verneinungen mit **be** bildest du so:

I **was** in New York.	Ich war in New York.
I **wasn't** in Washington.	Ich war nicht in Washington.
The Statue of Liberty **was** a present from France. It **wasn't** a present from Germany.	Die Freiheitsstatue war ein Geschenk von Frankreich. Sie war kein Geschenk von Deutschland.
We **were** in New York, but we **weren't** in Brooklyn.	Wir waren in New York, aber wir waren nicht in Brooklyn.

Fragen mit **be** bildest du so:

Were you at the zoo in Central Park?	Yes, I **was**.	No, I **wasn't**.
What **was** special in New York?	The Brooklyn Bridge.	

1 Say what they didn't do.

1. Matt lives in Manhattan now, but he *didn't live* ____________ there five years ago.
2. "Do you often watch TV?" – "Yes, but I ____________ anything yesterday."
3. Sally usually gives me nice birthday presents, but last year she ____________ me anything!
4. I often wear my red scarf, but I ____________ it yesterday.
5. I ate all my sandwiches, but Carrie ____________ her hot dog.

2 Say what they did.

buy | have | dance | play | look at ✓ | take

1. John and Mike looked at the Statue of Liberty ______ .
2. A man ______ .
3. Ken and Susan ______ .
4. Dean ______ .
5. Joanne ______ .
6. Lena and her friends ______ to music in Central Park.

3 Match the questions and answers.

1. Did David speak English as a child? → B
2. Where were David's parents born?
3. When did David become a taxi driver?
4. Did the tourists see New York in the snow?
5. Who did David tell about Nick's hot dogs?
6. Why did the trip to Manhattan take a long time?
7. What did David talk to his passenger about?
8. Did you enjoy your taxi ride?

A Ten years ago.
B Yes, he did.
C He talked about New York.
D He told one of his passengers.
E Yes, I did.
F In India.
G No, they didn't.
H There was a lot of traffic.

4 Complete the questions.

1. Did ______ the boys go ______ out yesterday? – Yes, they did. They went to Manhattan.
2. ______ they ______ the house? – They left at nine o'clock.
3. ______ a taxi? – No, they didn't. They took a bus.
4. ______? – They saw One World Trade Center and Times Square.
5. ______ anything? – Oh yes! They bought lots of souvenirs.
6. ______ a meal? – They had a meal in a small café.
7. ______? – They ordered pizza, salad and coke.
8. ______ any photos? – Yes, they did. They sent me this photo. Look!

5 Make questions.

a) Put the words in the right order.

1. did • to • the USA? • When • Marco's family • come

   When did Marco's family come to the USA?

2. first job? • What • his • was • grandfather's

   ______

3. restaurant? • Marco's parents • did • Where • open • their first

   ______

   ______

4. spicy • in • interested • food? • Were • New Yorkers

   ______

5. a waiter • didn't • Why • become • at the restaurant? • Marco

   ______

   ______

b) Find the right answers and write them down.

Queens | want • become • doctor | builder • Manhattan | yes • love it | 1930 ✓

1. They came in 1930.
2. ______
3. ______
4. ______
5. ______

6 Write the dialogue between Henry and Jake. Use the notes.

Henry: you • born • New York? *Were you born in New York?*

Jake: Queens • 2001 ______

Henry: where • you • go • school? ______

Jake: Queens • 4 years • then family • move • Manhattan ______

______

Henry: why • parents • move? ______

______

Jake: mother • get • good job • theater ______

______

7 What's that in English?

1. Gestern habe ich Steve getroffen. ______
2. Er hat mir von seiner Familie erzählt. ______
3. Vor zwanzig Jahren hat seine Mutter Deutschland verlassen.
   ______
4. Ich fragte: „Warum wollte deine Mutter nicht in Deutschland bleiben?"
   ______
   ______
5. Steve antwortete: „Sie bekam einen guten Job in New York.
   ______
   ______
6. Nach einer Woche in dieser Stadt hat sie beschlossen, hier zu bleiben!"
   ______
   ______

8 Ask four questions about the Statue of Liberty.

You need the simple present and the simple past.

1. *Who gave the Statue of Liberty to America?* – The people of France.
2. ______ – In New York Harbor.
3. ______ – In 1886.
4. ______ – No – a symbol of hope.

G2 Die Vorvergangenheit

The past perfect

Um über Ereignisse zu sprechen, die noch **vor** einem vergangenen Ereignis stattfanden, verwendest du die Vorvergangenheit, das **past perfect: had / hadn't + 3. Form** des Verbs (past participle).

Signalwörter	
after	nachdem
before	bevor

Bei den meisten Verben hängst du für die 3. Form ein **-ed** an das Verb: visit → **visited**
Achte auf unregelmäßige Verben, z. B. go → **gone**; see → **seen**; be → **been** etc.

Eine Liste der unregelmäßigen Verben findest du ab Seite 79.

Was in der Vergangenheit weiter zurückliegt, wird mit dem **past perfect** ausgedrückt!

She wasn't at home. She **had gone** to Tim's (house).	Sie war nicht zu Hause. Sie war zu Tim gegangen.
After I **had been** in NYC for two months, I moved to Chicago.	Nachdem ich zwei Monate in NYC gewesen war, zog ich nach Chicago um.
I **hadn't seen** skyscrapers before I went to New York.	Ich hatte noch keine Wolkenkratzer gesehen, bevor ich nach New York ging.

Und so kannst du im **past perfect** Fragen stellen:

Had you ever **been** to the USA before you left Cuba?	Yes, I **had**.	No, I **hadn't**.
Which countries **had** you **visited** before you went to the USA?	I **hadn't visited** any other countries at all.	

1 Complete the table.

infinitive	simple past	past participle
1. see	*saw*	seen
2. take	took	________
3. arrive	________	arrived
4. buy	bought	________
5. put	________	put
6. leave	________	left
7. watch	watched	________
8. be	was, were	________
9. go	________	gone
10. do	did	________
11. have	________	had

2 What had they done before? Finish the sentences.

1. take

2. send

3. eat

4. make

5. wash

6. play

1. Before Tom went shopping, he had taken the dog for a walk ____________.
2. Before Sally had dinner, ____________.
3. Before Mick and José watched a movie, ____________.
4. Before Mrs Lee opened her café, ____________.
5. Before Lizzie met her friends, ____________.
6. Before the boys took the subway, ____________.

3 What had Marco done before he went to the baseball game? What hadn't he done? Make sentences.

- write this week's blog ✓
- tidy up kitchen ✗
- check e-mails ✗
- order pizza for dinner ✓
- close windows ✗
- put on warm jacket ✓

1. Before Marco went to the baseball game, he had written this week's blog ____________, but he ____________ ____________.
2. ____________ ____________ ____________.
3. ____________ ____________.

4 Say what Amy did later.

a) Complete the sentences.

buy | call ✓ | cook | eat | put on | watch

1. First Amy called Tina ______________________.
2. After she had called Tina, ______________________.
3. After she ______________________.
4. ______________________ ______________________.
5. ______________________ ______________________ with Tina.
6. After Amy and Tina ______________________.

● b) Write three more sentences about Amy and Tina in your exercise book.
After Amy and Tina …

5 Match the questions and answers. Draw lines.

1. Why didn't you buy a DVD? → C
2. Had you been to New York before?
3. What did you have for lunch?
4. Did José find his phone?
5. When did Kate move to the UK?
6. Where had they seen skyscrapers before?

A Yes, he had left it in his hotel room.
B In London last year.
C I had spent all my money.
D No, that was my first trip.
E A salad which I had bought earlier.
F A few months after she had left school.

6 Interview The Cubans.

a) Write questions.

1. why • decide • leave • Cuba • after • finish • school?
   Raoul, why did you decide to leave Cuba after you had finished school ?
2. decide • become • singer • before • come • New York?
   José, ____________________ ?
3. learn • speak • English • before • leave • Cuba?
   Miguel, ____________________
   ____________________ ?
4. after • arrive • New York • how • get • money?
   Pablo, ____________________
   ____________________ ?

● b) Write your text with The Cubans' answers. Use your notes.

1. After Raoul had finished school he decided to leave Cuba because he wanted to become famous.
2. ____________________
   ____
   ____
3. ____________________
   ____
4. ____________________
   ____

1. Raoul:
   want • become • famous ✓
2. José:
   become singer • 14 years
3. Miguel:
   a little English • school
4. Pablo:
   work • clubs and cafés

● 7 Simple past or past perfect? Put in the right form.

1. After Tom had read (read) the message, he called (call) the hospital.
2. He ____________ (not hear) about the accident before Amy ____________ (tell) him.
3. The boys ____________ (go) to Julie's party after they ____________ (buy) her a present.
4. After we ____________ (live) in the USA for some time, we ____________ (speak) English well.
5. Before Lisa ____________ (become) a famous singer, she ____________ (work) in a café.
6. After Lisa ____________ (go) to the recording studio to make her first CD, she ____________ (feel) very excited.

8 Complete the sentences with the past perfect.

buy | eat ✓ | feed | read | spend | take

1 

2 

3 

4 

5 

6 

1. After Josh had eaten a sandwich ________________, he went out.
2. Mike ________________________ before he ate his breakfast.
3. Before Jenny visited New York, she ________________________________.
4. We couldn't buy any movie tickets because ________________________________.
5. The boys ________________________________ before they went to the party.
6. After the friends ________________________________, they sent it to their parents.

9 Find the right order. Number the sentences 1 – 9.

Alice

- Why were you so busy? School had finished a month ago. [ ]
- Ugh! I hate rice! Well, make sure you come to the club next week! [ ]
- You didn't come to drama club yesterday. Why not? [1]
- How did you help him? [ ]
- You're awful! You had had lots of time to learn them! [ ]

Bill

- Because I hadn't learned my lines. [2]
- School wasn't a problem. But my brother asked me to help him in his shop. [ ]
- Yes, I know, but I was very busy last week. [ ]
- Oh, I carried boxes. He had ordered lots of things – pasta, sugar, rice, … [ ]

● 10 Answer the questions. Use the past perfect.

1. How did Lenny know all the answers? (check • internet)

   He had checked them on the internet.

2. Why wasn't Matt at Sue's party? (not invite)

3. What did Maria show you? (T-shirt • she • buy • New York)

4. Why didn't Amy call us? (lose • number)

5. Why didn't Steve eat in the café? (eat dinner • home)

6. Why did so many people go to Marylou's concert? (see • her • TV)

11 What's that in English or German?

a) Write the sentences in German.

1. Pablo had already learned to speak English before he came to New York.

2. He lived with his parents because he hadn't found a flat.

3. Before Pablo became a doctor, he had worked in an office.

● **b)** Write the sentences in English.

1. Danny war oft nach New York gereist.

2. Wir hatten keine Fahrkarten gekauft.

3. Hattest du mich angerufen?

4. Viele Touristen hatten das neue Museum (noch) nicht gesehen.

1 Simple past or past perfect? Put in the right form.

1. I didn't take any photos because I had left (leave) my phone at home.
2. Mandy had already moved to New York when she ________ (call) me in April.
3. Lennie bought lots of new clothes because he ________ (win) some money in a competition.
4. Mario ________ (not check) his e-mails before he started work.
5. After the rain had stopped, people ________ (start) to play games in the park again.
6. We ________ (forget) our sports clothes, so we couldn't play on the team.

2 Ask Anita questions. Use the past perfect.

Before you started to make jewellery, Anita:

1. (Where • live?) Where had you lived?
2. (you • work • with people?) ________
3. (What • be • job?) ________
4. (you • meet many tourists?) ________
5. (When • become interested • jewellery?) ________
6. (you • spend • money • jewellery?) ________

3 Match the questions and answers. Draw lines.

1. When did you tell Emma about the hip-hop concert?
2. Why didn't Josh play on the team?
3. Did you enjoy the movie?
4. Where did Dad find his phone?
5. Why wasn't Mike at the concert?
6. Did the taxi driver speak English well?

A Yes – but I had seen it before.
B Because he had forgotten to buy a ticket.
C Yes, of course! He had come to New York from England!
D After I had read about it on the internet.
E On the table – where he had left it!
F Because he had broken his leg.

4 Look at Amy's diary for last Monday and complete the sentences.

1. Before Amy met the tourists at their hotel, she *had taken the subway to Manhattan*.
2. After ______________________ the sights in Manhattan, she ______________________ .
3. After ______________ lunch, she ______________________ with a German group.
4. Before she ______________ at the movie theater, she ______________________ .

MONDAY
- 9:00 a.m. take subway to Manhattan
- 10:30 a.m. meet tourists at hotel
- 11:00 a.m. show tourists the sights of Manhattan
- 1:30 p.m. have lunch with Henry
- 3:00 p.m. visit Statue of Liberty with German group
- 6:00 p.m. call Mr Leroy at office
- 8:15 p.m. meet Henry at movie theater

5 Read the text. Find the right order and number the pictures 1 – 4.

On Wednesday morning Matt wanted to ride his bike to the supermarket to buy some pasta. But before that he had to take his dog Fraser for a walk. Fraser was very slow, so when he got home again, his mother said, "Where's that pasta? I'm waiting for it!"
"Sorry, I'm on my way now," Matt said and got on his bike. After he had bought the pasta he left the supermarket.
On his way home he remembered. – The day before he had found a small bag under a tree. After he had given the bag to the police, he took the pasta home to his mother.

☐

☐

☐

☐

6 Simple past or past perfect? Put in the right form.

On the first day of Laura's visit to New York her aunt and uncle *took* (take) her to the top of the Empire State Building. Laura ______________ (never see) so many skyscrapers before! Her uncle ______________ (show) her the Rockefeller Center. That's where he ______________ (work) before he ______________ (get) a job at a museum. Before Laura ______________ (come) to New York, she ______________ (look) at some websites with fantastic photos of New York. But when she ______________ (stand) on the top of a skyscraper, the scene ______________ (be) even better than she ______________ (think).

G3 Modale Hilfsverben und ihre Ersatzformen

Modal auxiliaries and their substitutes

Modale Hilfsverben kannst du nur im **simple present** verwenden. Für alle anderen Zeiten, benötigst du **Ersatzformen.** Ausnahme **can**: Für **can** kannst du im **simple past** auch **could** verwenden.

Mit **can / could** und der Ersatzform **be able to** sagst du, was du tun **kannst** (Fähigkeit).

Simple present	Simple past
Kim **can / is able to** speak English.	Kim **could / was able to** understand it.
Kim **kann** Englisch sprechen.	Kim **konnte** es verstehen.
Can he / **Is** he **able to** speak English?	**Could** he / **Was** he **able to** speak English?
Kann er Englisch sprechen?	**Konnte** er Englisch sprechen?

Mit **can / could** und der Ersatzform **be allowed to** sagst du, was du tun **darfst** (Erlaubnis).

She **can't / isn't allowed to** use her phone.	She **couldn't / wasn't allowed to** use it.
Sie **darf** ihr Handy **nicht** benutzen.	Sie **durfte** es **nicht** benutzen.
Can you / **Are** you **allowed to** wear jeans?	**Could** you / **Were** you **allowed to** wear jeans?
Darfst du Jeans tragen?	**Durftest** du Jeans tragen?

Mit **must** und der Ersatzform **have to** sagst du, was du tun **musst** (Verpflichtung).

Sarah **must** take English and History.	Sarah **had to** take Biology too.
Sarah **muss** Englisch und Geschichte nehmen.	Sarah **musste** auch Biologie nehmen.
We **don't have to** worry.	We **didn't have to** worry.
Wir **müssen** uns **keine** Sorgen machen.	Wir **mussten** uns **keine** Sorgen machen.
Must you help your parents?	**Did** you **have to** help in the house?
Musst du deinen Eltern helfen?	**Musstest** du im Haus helfen?

Bei **must** musst du die Ersatzform schon in **verneinten Sätzen** im **simple present** benutzen!

1 Complete the dialogue. Use was/were (not) allowed to.

Sue: We *were allowed to have* ________ (have) a party at school last week. But we ________ (not • invite) students from other schools.

Dan: ________ (you • bring) Jacob?

Sue: No, he ________ (not • come). He doesn't go to our school.

Dan: And Ashley ________ (not • buy) a new skirt. Is that right?

Sue: Yes. – Her mum said no. But she ________ (borrow) a skirt from her big sister.

2 What was Martin able to do? Complete the sentences. Use the simple past.

1. During my student exchange last year I was able to meet __________ (meet) lots of interesting people.
2. The kids in my exchange family __________ (help) me with my English homework.
3. But they __________ (not • understand) German.
4. After my first week Mrs Leroy asked me, "__________ (you • join) a school sports team, Martin?"
5. I said, "No, I __________ (not • play) well enough."
6. But I joined the Cooking Club, and soon __________ (make) delicious food!

3 What did Sven have to do during his exchange year?

1. get up • make
2. take • learn
3. take out • tidy up
4. go (to) • take

1. Sven had to get up at 6:30, but __________.
2. He __________ __________.
3. __________ __________.
4. __________ __________.

4 Write about the past. Use the past tense.

a) Complete the sentences.

1. When Luise was a child, she *had to* ____________ (have to) go to bed early.
2. She ____________ (not allow to) go shopping alone.
3. When Luise was older, her parents ____________ (not have to) take her to school.
4. When she was 14, she ____________ (allow to) see movies with friends.
5. She and her friends ____________ (allow to) go on a class trip to England.
6. When Luise was in the USA for her exchange year, she ____________ (not have to) pay for her food.

b) What about you? Complete the sentences.

1. When I was younger, I had to *go to bed early* ____________ .
2. But I was allowed to ____________ .
3. I had to ____________ .
4. But I didn't have to ____________ .
5. I wasn't allowed to ____________ .
6. But I was allowed to ____________
____________ .

• 5 Complete the text. Use (not) able to, (not) allowed to or (not) have to.

I had a terrible dream last night! I was in a big room with a monster, and I *had to* ____________ do what it told me. There was lots of food on a table, but I ____________ eat anything. I found a door, but I ____________ open it. – It was too heavy. Then the monster brought me a bagel and I ____________ ____________ eat it. After some time I escaped, but I ____________ ____________ run fast enough. The monster was behind me! Then I woke up. I ____________ run. I was safe in my bed.

6 Write sentences in the simple past.

1. You must clean your shoes, Lennie.
2. You can invite some friends, if you like.
3. You can't carry that box. It's too big.
4. You don't have to help with dinner.
5. You can't see that movie. It's for adults only.
6. But you can play a video game.

Yes, Mum.

1. Lennie had to clean his shoes ______ .
2. He ______ friends.
3. He ______ . It was too big.
4. He ______ .
5. He ______ . It was for adults only.
6. But he ______ play a video game.

7 What's that in English or German?

a) Write the sentences in German.

1. They were allowed to wear jeans.

______

2. We had to answer lots of questions.

______

3. Andy couldn't find his phone.

______

4. Did you have to buy a ticket?

______

b) Write the sentences in English.

1. Ich musste nicht lange warten.

______

2. Ich konnte einige Wörter nicht verstehen.

______

3. Wir durften keinen Schmuck tragen.

______

4. Konntest du die hohen Berge sehen?

______

G4 R: Bedingungssätze Typ I

Revision: If-clauses type I

Um Bedingungen und Folgen auszudrücken, benutzt man **if**-**Sätze**.
Dabei steht im **if-Satz** das **simple present**, im Hauptsatz das **will-future**.
Geht der **if**-Satz voran, steht am Ende des **if**-Satzes ein Komma.

Bedingung (condition)	Folge (consequence)	
If Michael **finds** a job,	he **will earn** some money.	Wenn Michael einen Job findet, wird er etwas Geld verdienen.
If you **don't work** well,	you **won't get** a bonus.	Wenn du nicht gut arbeitest, bekommst du keine Prämie.

Bedingungssätze können auch mit dem Hauptsatz beginnen. Dann entfällt das Komma.

Folge (consequence)	Bedingung (condition)	
You **will be** late	if you **walk.**	Du wirst zu spät kommen, wenn du zu Fuß gehst.
You **won't be** successful	if you **don't work** more carefully.	Du wirst nicht erfolgreich sein, wenn du nicht sorgfältiger arbeitest.

Das **will-future** drückt allgemein Zukünftiges aus. Im **if**-Satz steht nie **will** oder **won't**!

Für das **will-future** kannst du im Deutschen die Zukunft oder die Gegenwart benutzen. Beides ist richtig. Vergleiche:

He will earn some money.	Er wird etwas Geld verdienen. Er verdient etwas Geld.

1 Put in the right form of the verb.

1. If Tina *gets* __________ (get) a weekend job, she will have more money to spend.
2. Her boss will give her extra money if she __________ (sell) lots of expensive clothes.
3. Steve __________ (lose) his job if he's late again.
4. If a customer steals something, we __________ (call) the police.
5. If Jane __________ (have) any problems, she'll ask a co-worker.
6. She will try to stay polite if customers __________ (not buy) anything.
7. Tina's parents will be surprised if she __________ (not spend) her extra money on new shoes.
8. If you buy this special offer, you __________ (pay) only ten dollars.
9. Tina won't play for her team if there __________ (be) a game on Saturday.
10. Students __________ (not do) well at school if they work 20 hours a week.

2 Match the sentence parts.

1. If you like animals, → D
2. My co-workers will help me
3. If William buys all those new clothes,
4. If the boss is pleased with Marie's work,
5. You'll have to go out in bad weather
6. If Madison wants to pay for her driver's license,

A if you become a dog walker.
B she'll give her more money.
C if I don't know what to do.
D you'll enjoy your job as a dog walker.
E she'll have to get a weekend job.
F he won't have any money for his car.

3 Look at the pictures. Complete the sentences.

1. If Andrew needs some money, he'll ask his grandparents.
2. Emma will buy a new bike if ______.
3. The friends won't play baseball ______.
4. If Laura has to wear a silly uniform, ______.
5. If Michael is unfriendly to the customers, ______.
6. Sarah will borrow her parents' car ______.

4 Put in the right words.

aren't | will be | will spend | asks | doesn't get | will get

1. If the boss gives me more money, I will spend it on a holiday.
2. Amy ______ better grades at school if she goes to bed earlier.
3. If Olivia gets a weekend job in a café, her friends ______ very jealous.
4. If Jacob ______ good grades at school, he'll give up his weekend job.
5. Danny will be sad if his friends ______ interested in his new job.
6. If a customer ______ difficult questions, the boss will try to answer them.

5 Complete the sentences. Use the notes.

1. If Jacob is sick, *he'll see a doctor* .
2. Emma's friends will be surprised if ____________ .
3. Her parents will give her some money if ____________ .
4. If Jacob has a party, ____________ .
5. If Julia gets her driver's license, ____________ .
6. Jacob won't enjoy his work if ____________ .

1. see • doctor ✓
2. give up • job
3. need • new shoes
4. invite • all friends
5. borrow • parents' car
6. have to carry • boxes

● 6 What's that in English?

1. Wenn ich Zeit habe, rufe ich dich an. ____________
2. Matt wird einen Job im Sportgeschäft bekommen, wenn er sich bald bewirbt. ____________
3. Wenn ein Kunde etwas stiehlt, wird der Manager die Polizei rufen. ____________
4. Ashley wird viel Geld im Laden ausgeben, wenn es Sonderangebote gibt. ____________

● 7 Complete the dialogue with if or when.

Tyler: Are you going to work in the sports store today, Andy?

Andy: Yes, I am. I start work there at 5 p.m.

Tyler: *When* you get there, will you look at the "T-Star" T-shirts for me?

Andy: OK; I'll do that – ____________ the boss doesn't have other plans for me.

Tyler: Great! ____________ there's a blue T-shirt in size 'M', can you buy it for me?

Andy: OK – but only ____________ you promise to give me the money tomorrow!

Tyler: Sure! I'll give it to you ____________ I see you at school. We have the first class together, remember?

Andy: Right, see you tomorrow, Tyler.

G5 Stützwort one / ones

One / ones

Um eine unnötige Wiederholung von Nomen zu vermeiden, kannst du sie durch **one** (Einzahl) und **ones** (Mehrzahl) ersetzen. **One / ones** werden nicht übersetzt. Sie stehen oft nach einem Adjektiv. Auch nach der Steigerungsform eines Adjektivs kommt **one** oder **ones** häufig vor.

Who are those boys over there?	Wer sind diese Jungs dort drüben?
The tall ~~boy~~ **one** is Jim and the short ~~boy~~ **one** is Tim.	Der große ~~Junge~~ ist Jim und der kleine ~~Junge~~ ist Tim.
Which towels did you buy?	Welche Handtücher hast du gekauft?
– The cheaper **ones.**	– Die billigeren.
Which books do you prefer?	Welche Bücher bevorzugst du?
– Exciting **ones.**	– Spannende.

One oder **ones** stehen auch oft nach Fragen mit **which.**

You can borrow my CDs.	Du kannst dir meine CDs ausleihen.
Which ones would you like?	**Welche** möchtest du?
There are lots of nice T-shirts here.	Es gibt hier viele schöne T-Shirts.
Which one do you like best?	**Welches** gefällt dir am besten?

1 Complete the sentences with one or ones.

1. Which ball would you like? – I'd like the red _one_ ________, please.
2. Do you eat lots of apples? – Yes, I do. Green __________ and red __________ .
3. Can I help you? – Yes, you can. I'm looking for a T-shirt – a white __________ .
4. These bags are awesome! – Well, that pink __________ is OK.
5. Can you go and buy some bagels? Nice fresh __________ , please!
6. The tall boy over there is Jacob and the short __________ is Daniel.

2 Complete the answers with one or ones. Write one/ones if both words are right.

1. You can borrow a torch, if you want. Which _one_ __________ would you like?
2. Look at all the exciting DVDs! Which ________________ should I choose?
3. We found three phones in the school bus. Which ______________ is yours?
4. Can you help me to choose some sports shoes, please. Which ______________ are the best?
5. Hannah has lots of T-shirts. Which ___________ look really cool?
6. I can't decide between these two student jobs. Which ______________ would you choose?
7. Ryan has bought a lot of magazines. Which ________________ will he give to his girlfriend?
8. Sarah has two part-time jobs. Which ____________ did she start last week?

3 Complete the dialogues.

1. black

2. big

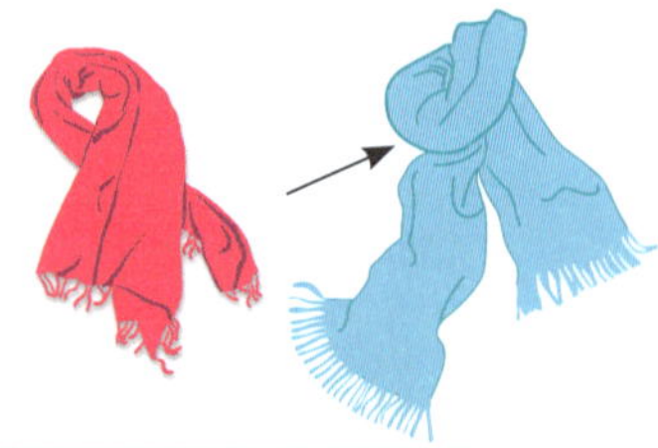

3. long

4. exciting

5. tall

6. cheaper

1. Which sports shoes do you want to buy? – The black ones.
2. Do you like dogs? – Oh yes! Especially ______ .
3. Have you chosen a scarf yet? – Yes, I'd like ______ , please.
4. Are you looking for a good comic? – Yes, I am. Do you have a really ______ ?
5. Are those two boys your brothers? – Those two boys? No, just ______ .
6. These clothes are very fashionable this year. – The dresses are nice, but do you have any ______ ?

4 Correct the sentences. Put in one or ones.

1. You've just eaten my bagel! – Sorry. I'll get you another ~~bagel~~. one
2. I don't like this movie. It's not as exciting as the movies we saw last week. ______
3. Can you sort these T-shirts for me, please? Put the blue T-shirts on the left and the white T-shirts on the right. This green T-shirt can go into the sale. ______ ______
4. I'm so sad that I missed Emma's party. She won't have another party for a long time. ______
5. These bags are very expensive. Do you want to buy a bag? – I really need a new bag. I think I'll get that small bag. ______ ______
6. That's a great skirt, Olivia! I don't usually like long skirts, but that skirt is cool! ______

5 Find the right order. Number the sentences 1 – 8.

Hannah		Emily	
But I already have a blue jacket. I don't want another one.	☐	A scarf? Let's look at those long ones there. Maybe I'll buy one for myself. Come on, Hannah!	☐
I really need a new jacket, Emily.	1	Red isn't your colour. It doesn't suit you. What about the blue jackets over there?	☐
Yes, I hadn't thought of my jeans. This jacket fits me really well. Now I just need a warm scarf.	☐	A jacket for the winter? There are some nice warm ones here.	☐
Yes, you're right. They're very warm. What do you think of this red one?	☐	Please, Hannah, just try this blue one on. It will go well with your jeans.	☐

● 6 Make dialogues.

- Which one is more exciting?
- What about the old ones?
- Which ones fit better? ✓
- Do you like this green one?
- The one on the right.
- No, I like the one with the flowers.
- They're broken.
- The pink ones. ✓

1 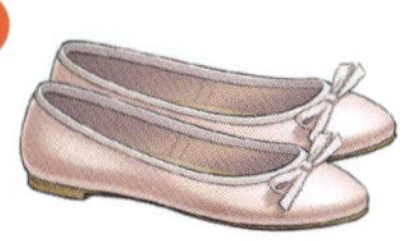
2 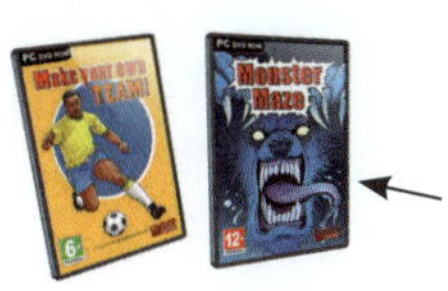
3 
4 

1. Which ones fit better? – The pink ones.
2. ______________________
3. ______________________
4. ______________________

● 7 What's that in English?

1. Welches T-Shirt möchtest du? – Das gelbe.
____
2. Mein neues Fahrrad ist besser als mein altes.
____
3. Martins Schuhe sind zu klein. Er braucht neue.
____

1 Complete the sentences.

was allowed to | had to (2x) ✓ | weren't allowed to | didn't have to | were allowed to | wasn't allowed to

1. When Emma was younger, she _had to_ walk to school because there was no school bus.
2. We ______ make any noise because Grandma was asleep.
3. In the past everyone ______ visit the cave, but now there's a sign that says "Keep out!".
4. I ______ buy a ticket because my friend had two.
5. Ashley ______ invite more than eight friends to the party. – Her mum's rule!
6. The girls were lucky. They ______ join the cheerleaders.
7. Two years ago Marco ______ ask for help with his homework, but now he can do it alone.

2 Put in the right form of the verb.

1. If William _stays_ (stay) in bed until seven o'clock, he'll be late for school.
2. He ______ (not have) time to put his books in his locker if he doesn't leave now.
3. If he leaves the classroom without a hall pass, he ______ (get) extra homework.
4. William will play in an important football game next week if he ______ (not forget) his equipment.
5. If Madison comes to school in a short skirt, her teacher ______ (give) her a note for her parents.
6. "Madison, if you don't like our school rules, you ______ (have to) find another school."
7. If Madison ______ (join) the cheerleaders, she'll go to lots of great football games.
8. She'll be sad if her friends ______ (not like) her uniform.

● 3 Complete the sentences. Use these words or your own ideas.

room | money | friends ✓ | family | ...

1. If my parents go out this evening, _I'll invite my friends to our house_.
2. I'll look for a weekend job if ______.
3. If I have lots of free time this weekend, ______.
4. I'll go on an exchange to the USA next year if ______.

4 Find the right order. Number the sentences 1 – 10.

Tyler		Joshua	
I'll certainly ask him! Let's meet at the café in town.		He's my cousin. You know, the one from New York City.	
Hi, Josh! I have an idea. – Let's meet in town tomorrow.	1	Sure, that's great. We'll be there at four o'clock – if I don't forget!	
The one with the burgers, if that's OK with you. Let's meet at four o'clock.		Good idea! But if I meet you in town, I'll have to bring Ethan with me.	
He was an exchange student in England, right?		The Italian one or the one that sells those awesome burgers?	
Ethan? Who's he?		That's right. He was in London. He'll tell you all about it if you ask him.	

● 5 Complete the text.

be able | was allowed | had | one (2x) | ones | survive | were ✓ | will | work

Emily: Hi there! I'm Emily.

Daniel: Hello Emily. I'm Daniel and I've just started a part-time job here.

Emily: Nice to meet you Daniel. How was your interview with the manager? I guess you *were* able to impress him.

Daniel: But the interview was tough! I ________ to answer lots of questions and I wasn't allowed to think about my answers for very long. If I ____________ my first day here, I'll be happy.

Emily: Don't worry. If you have any problems, you ________ find people who can help you.

Daniel: Will I get a bonus if I ________ well?

Emily: Maybe. Last month I ______________________ to choose a new T-shirt from the store. I chose this ________.

Daniel: It's cool! What are the customers like here?

Emily: Well, there are the nice ________ – and there are the people who complain.

Daniel: Will I __________________ to behave correctly with the difficult people?

Emily: Sure! Just remember the staff rules. The most important ________ is: the customer is always right.

Language tip

G6 Bestätigungsfragen

Question tags

Um ein Gespräch nicht abreißen zu lassen, kannst du eine Bestätigungsfrage (question tag) benutzen. Im Deutschen sagt man dafür Ausdrücke wie **nicht wahr?**, **nicht?**, **oder?**
Für negative **question tags** benutzt du immer Kurzformen.
Alle **question tags** werden mit einem Komma vom Aussagesatz abgetrennt.

Ist der Aussagesatz positiv **+**, so wird die Bestätigungsfrage negativ **–**.

Aussagesatz +	Question tag –
It's cold,	**isn't** it?
You **are** fifteen,	**aren't** you?
She **can** play the guitar,	**can't** she?
Robert **was** in Boston,	**wasn't** he?
You **were** in New York,	**weren't** you?

Ist der Aussagesatz negativ **–**, so wird die Bestätigungsfrage positiv **+**.

Aussagesatz –	Question tag +
Your shirt **isn't** new,	**is** it?
You **weren't** in the USA last year,	**were** you?

Bei Vollverben musst du **do**, **does**, **did** oder **don't**, **doesn't**, **didn't** benutzen:

You **like** chocolates,	**don't** you?
Julia **wants** to go to Miami,	**doesn't** she?
You **met Brenda**,	**didn't** you?
You **don't like** turkey,	**do** you?
Nick **doesn't drink** coke,	**does** he?
Robert **didn't see** the Niagara Falls,	**did** he?

1 Complete the sentences with the correct question tag.

1. You aren't from Boston, *are you* ?
2. The store wasn't open yesterday, ______ ?
3. I can borrow your phone, ______ ?
4. Joshua and Mary were at the party last week, ______ ?
5. Tyler can't speak German, ______ ?
6. Your T-shirt isn't very clean, ______ ?
7. You're Joshua's brother, ______ ?
8. We'll meet Bill at the concert, ______ ?
9. Tyler is Susan's boyfriend, ______ ?
10. Emily's party was awesome, ______ ?

2 Complete the sentences. Choose the correct question tag.

does she · doesn't she · do they · don't they · don't you · did you · didn't they · didn't we ✓

1. We all enjoyed the meal, didn't we ?
2. My sister doesn't eat a lot, ________________ ?
3. My grandma asks lots of questions, ________________ ?
4. You didn't meet her at Thanksgiving last year, ________________ ?
5. Most people watch the big game after dinner, ________________ ?
6. My parents gave our dog a very big turkey dinner, ________________ ?
7. Ryan and Amy don't visit their grandparents at Thanksgiving, ________________ ?
8. You want to send Matthew a text, ________________ ?

3 Complete the sentences. Look at the pictures and the question tags.

1. like

2. break

3. watch

4. buy

5. live

6. play

1. Bill doesn't like bananas, does he?
2. Hannah ________________, didn't she?
3. They ________________, did they?
4. Susan ________________, won't she?
5. You ________________, don't you?
6. Tyler ________________, can he?

4 What's that in German?

1. That's Brenda's car, isn't it? ______
2. You didn't leave my DVD at school, did you?
______
______
3. Tyler and Mick weren't on the football team last year, were they?
______
______
4. We'll see Joshua at the party, won't we?
______
______

• 5 Complete the sentences with the right question tags.

Noah: You know about Julia's problem, *don't you* ?

Emily: Yes, of course. She can't come to the game on Saturday afternoon.

Noah: That's right! She has to work at the sports store. She works every weekend, ______ ?
That's tough, ______ ? And she's one of our best cheerleaders.

Emily: Well, I guess she won't miss much. Our boys lost the last two games, ______ ?

Noah: Don't talk like that! Our players need all their fans – and their best cheerleaders.

Emily: Maybe Julia can work in the store on Friday evening – or on Saturday morning. It opens early,
______ ?

Noah: Yes, it does. Emily, you sometimes have great ideas, ______ ?
Let's talk to Julia!

• 6 Complete the sentences. Look at the pictures and the question tags.

1 

2 

3 

4 

1. Emma *is (very) happy* , isn't she?
2. Bill ______ , can he?
3. You ______ , didn't you?
4. The Watsons ______ , do they?

G7 R: Fragen

Revision: Questions / questions with who

So bildest du unterschiedliche Fragen mit Vollverben, z. B. like, go etc.:

Fragen, auf die man mit yes oder no antwortet (Ja/Nein-Fragen)
– Fragen im **simple present** beginnst du mit **do** oder **does** (he, she, it).

Do you **like** turkey?	Magst du Truthahn?
Does Jacob **like** chocolate?	Mag Jacob Schokolade?

– Fragen im **simple past** beginnst du mit **did** für alle Personen.

Did you **travel** by car last year?	Bist du letztes Jahr mit dem Auto verreist?
Did it **rain** last December?	Hat es im letzten Dezember geregnet?

– Fragen im **will-future** beginnst du mit **will** für alle Personen.

Will you **call** us again tomorrow?	Wirst du uns morgen nochmal anrufen?

Fragen mit Fragewörtern

What do you **like**?	Was magst du gerne?
Where did you **spend** your summer?	Wo hast du deinen Sommer verbracht?
When will you **go** to Boston?	Wann wirst du nach Boston fahren?

Fragen mit who
– Das Fragewort **who?** kann **verschiedene Bedeutungen** haben:
– Heißt es **Wer?** wird **keine Form von do** verwendet.
– Heißt es **Wen?** oder **Wem?** muss **eine Form von do** verwendet werden.

Who lives in Boston?	**Wer** lebt in Boston?
Who do you **like**?	**Wen** magst du?
Who did you **help** last week?	**Wem** hast du letzte Woche geholfen?

Präpositonen bleiben in Fragen meistens beim Verb stehen. Im Deutschen dagegen steht die Präposition meistens beim Fragewort. Vergleiche:

Who did you **talk to?**	**Mit wem** hast du dich unterhalten?
What do you **feel** thankful **for?**	**Wofür** bist du dankbar?

1 Make questions with do or does.

1. Do you like ______ (you • like) chocolate?
2. ______ (Julia • always • have) a lot of work?
3. ______ (I • need) a ticket for your concert?
4. ______ (it • usually • rain) on Thanksgiving?
5. ______ (Jacob's friends • send) him lots of texts?
6. ______ (Brenda • sometimes • come) by train?

2 Complete the questions.

Are the girls	Are your friends	Can you	Is your brother ✓
Was Emma's dress	Were you	Will you	Will your friends

1. Is your brother ______ watching TV? – Yes, he is.
2. ______ be at home this evening? – No, I won't.
3. ______ from Boston? – Yes, they are.
4. ______ play the saxophone? – No, I can't.
5. ______ in Boston last week? – Yes, I was.
6. ______ wait for you? – Yes, they will.
7. ______ expensive? – No, it wasn't.
8. ______ making dinner just now? – No, they aren't.

● 3 Complete the dialogue.

1. Did ______ Sarah and Olivia go to see ______ a movie yesterday? – Yes, they did. They went to see "The House of Secrets".
2. ______ ? – Oh yes! It was very scary!
3. ______ ? – No, they weren't. Sarah and Olivia are never scared!
4. The movie sounds great! ______ scary movies? – Yes, I like them very much.
5. ______ to see *The House of Secrets*? – Yes, OK. I'll come with you next Friday.
6. ______ tickets online? – Yes, we can buy them online.
7. ______ – No, that's a bit late. I'll meet you at half past two.

4 Match the questions and the answers.

1. Did I tell you about the storm last week? → C
2. Can I borrow your sports shoes?
3. Will your friends still be here tomorrow?
4. Can we cook pasta for dinner tonight?
5. Will you come to the party next month?
6. Did you see the game on TV?

A Yes, I did. But my team didn't win!
B Yes, good idea. And we can have a salad too.
C No, you didn't. Was the weather very bad?
D Of course I will! I never miss a celebration.
E No, sorry, you can't. I need them for the game.
F No, they won't. They have to go home soon.

5 Put a circle around the right question.

1. a) What did the Millers eat yesterday? (b) Were the Millers at home yesterday?)	Yes, they celebrated Thanksgiving together.
2. a) Where did Lily's plane have to land? b) When did Lily's plane arrive?	In New York.
3. a) What did Robert give to Julia? b) Who gave a present to Julia?	A box of chocolates.
4. a) When do Americans celebrate Thanksgiving? b) Why do Americans eat turkey on Thanksgiving?	At the end of November.

6 Look at the pictures. Complete the questions and write down the answers. Use the simple past.

1. Jacob • put

2. Julia • get up

3. the Millers • watch

4. Julia • get

5. Brenda • arrive

6. Jacob • eat

1. Where did Jacob put the turkey ? – On the table .
2. When ______ ? – ______ .
3. What ______ ? – ______ .
4. How many ______ ? – ______ .
5. When ______ ? – ______ .
6. What ______ ? – ______ .

7 Questions and answers

a) Put the words in the right order. Make questions.

1. do • the Millers • Why • invite • to their house • Robert • ?

   Why do the Millers invite Robert to their house?

2. Jacob • on Thanksgiving • eat • Why • doesn't • turkey • ?

   ______

3. again • Lily • her parents • will • call • When • ?

   ______

4. can • the Millers • after their meal • do • What • ?

   ______

● b) Write down the answers to the questions.

1. *Because he doesn't have family in Boston.*
2. ______
3. ______
4. ______

8 Find the right order. Number the sentences 1 – 8.

Joshua		Danny	
Oh, sorry, I forgot! Happy birthday! How many presents did you get?	☐	My parents gave it to me for my birthday. I don't know how much they paid for it.	☐
Hey, where did you get that awesome sports bag?	1	OK, I'll bring it to the sports club tomorrow.	☐
Yes, I would. I love comedy!	☐	At a store in town. Do you like it?	☐
Yes, I do. It's really cool. How much did it cost?	☐	Oh, – four or five. My brother gave me a DVD of his favourite comedy show. It's very funny. Would you like to borrow it?	☐

9 Read the text. Write down the questions.

Ashley was born in 2002. She started to play the guitar when she was eight years old and later she had music lessons in Boston. When she was twelve, she won the first prize in a competition. Now Ashley is 15 and she has won five prizes. In her free time she plays hip hop in a band.

1. When was Ashley born? – In 2002.
2. ______ – When she was eight years old.
3. ______ – In Boston.
4. ______ – The first prize in a competition.
5. ______ – Five.
6. ______ – Hip hop.

10 Put a circle around the right answer.

1. Who saw Amy in the park?	a) She saw the boys. b) Jacob saw her.
2. Who did the girls help?	a) They helped Mrs Miller. b) A friend helped them.
3. Who does Ryan phone after school?	a) He phones Susan. b) His football friends phone him.
4. Who gave Kate that box of chocolates?	a) She gave it to her mum. b) Her boyfriend gave it to her.

11 What's that in German?

1. Did the boys help in the kitchen?

______

2. When will the next train arrive?

______

3. Where can I buy a box of chocolates?

______

4. Were your grandparents at the family celebration last year?

______

5. Who can play music at our party?

______

6. Who did Madison see when she opened the door?

______

12 Put in do, does or did – if necessary.

1. Who ~~—~~ gave you my phone number?
2. Who ________ Matthew meet at the game yesterday?
3. Who ________ Amy like better: Tyler or Joshua?
4. Who ________ cooks all the meals in your family?
5. Who ________ you ask for help when you have problems with your homework?
6. Who ________ left my bike outside last night?

13 Ask questions about the underlined words.

1. Who did Jessica look after? – Jessica looked after her younger sister.
2. ________ – I'm looking for my phone.
3. ________ – Amy has fallen in love with Ethan.
4. ________ – My parents talked about Thanksgiving.
5. ________ – Emily usually asks for a coke and a bagel.
6. ________ – We must wait for our visitors.
7. ________ – My grandma listens to this kind of music.
8. ________ – Susan put on her new dress.

14 What's that in English?

1. Wann stehst du jeden Morgen auf?

____

2. Wo wird Max seinen Urlaub verbringen?

____

3. Wen hat Sophie letztes Jahr besucht?

____

4. Hast du gestern die Fotos im Internet gesehen?

____

G8 R: Bedingungssätze Typ II

Revision: If-clauses type II

Bei den Bedingungssätzen Typ II ist eine Bedingung unwahrscheinlich oder nicht erfüllbar.
Du verwendest im **if-Satz simple past**. Im Hauptsatz steht **would / wouldn't + Grundform des Verbs**.

Bedingung (condition)	Folge (consequence)	
If it **rained**,	I **would stay** at home.	Wenn es regnen würde, würde ich zu Hause bleiben.
If you **didn't call**,	I **would be** very sad.	Wenn du nicht anrufen würdest, wäre ich sehr traurig.

Bedingungssätze können auch mit dem Hauptsatz beginnen. Dann entfällt das Komma.

Folge (consequence)	Bedingung (condition)	
I **would buy** new clothes	if I **had** more money.	Ich würde mir neue Kleidung kaufen, wenn ich genug Geld hätte.
I **wouldn't have** problems with my clothes	if I **lived** in the Amish community.	Ich hätte keine Kleidungsprobleme, wenn ich in der Gemeinschaft der Amish leben würde.

Statt **If I was** … wird oft **If I were** … gebraucht.

If I **were** a film star,	I **would live** in Beverley Hills.	Wenn ich ein Filmstar wäre, würde ich in Beverly Hills wohnen.

Im **if-Satz** steht nie **would / wouldn't**!

Im Deutschen verwendet man in beiden Satzteilen **würde**, **wäre** oder **hätte (Konjunktiv)**.

1 Put in the right form of the verb.

1. If Emma *had* ________ (have) more time, she would visit her grandparents more often.
2. Ryan would do more jobs around the house if his parents ________________ (ask) him.
3. Tom's friends would be surprised if he ________________ (buy) a saxophone.
4. If I ______________________ (not phone) Tyler so often, I wouldn't know all the gossip.
5. The girls would miss a lot of fun if they ________________ (not be) in the sports club.

2 Put in the right form of the verb.

1. If the weather wasn't so bad, we *would go* ____________ (go) out this afternoon.
2. Amy ______________________ (not be) happy if her boyfriend moved to another town.
3. I ____________________ (buy) a new computer if I had enough money.
4. If Mike broke his phone, he ________________________ (not know) what to do.
5. If the girls wore short skirts to school, their teacher ____________________ (send) them home.

3 Look at the pictures. Complete the sentences.

buy | not eat | get up | live ✓ | not play | drink

1. Joshua would go to school on the subway if he lived in New York .
2. Ashley's parents would be angry if ______________________ .
3. If Sarah had 10,000 dollars, ______________________ .
4. The boys would find life boring if ______________________ .
5. If Jessica didn't have school today, ______________________ .
6. If the Smiths were vegetarians, ______________________ .

4 Match the sentence parts.

1. If Jennifer lived in Germany, → C
2. Ruth would have to start a new life
3. We would buy a present for the Millers
4. If the girls had a car,
5. If Ethan had a microwave,
6. We would miss all our modern devices

A if we joined the Amish community.
B he would make popcorn.
C she wouldn't celebrate Thanksgiving.
D they wouldn't go to school by bus.
E if she didn't go back to her family.
F if they invited us to their Thanksgiving dinner.

5 Complete the dialogue with the right verb forms.

Dad: It's after seven o'clock, Austin. If you didn't have (not have) to do everything so quickly every morning, you would have time for a good breakfast.

Austin: True, Dad. But I ______________ (eat) a bigger breakfast if I didn't have to run for the school bus. You see, Dad – if you ______________ (take) me to school by car, I would enjoy my breakfast.

Dad: You're forgetting something. If I took you to school at seven o'clock, I ______________ (be) late for work. If you ______________ (get up) so late, …

Austin: OK, OK, Dad!

6 Put in the right verb forms.

had	wouldn't have	wasn't	wouldn't be ✓
found	wouldn't find		

1. Ruth's family _wouldn't be_ happy if she decided to leave the community.
2. If Jennifer ______ a driver's license, she would take her friends to the movies by car.
3. Ruth ______ life easy if she went to live in a big city.
4. If Jennifer ______ interested in fashion, she wouldn't think about clothes so often.
5. The girls ______ time to chat together for hours if they worked in a store.
6. If Jennifer ______ an interesting website about the Amish, she would probably read it.

7 Complete the sentences.

a) Use the notes to complete the sentences.

1. Madison would buy a car if _she had a driver's license_. (have • driver's license)
2. If we went to Pennsylvania, ______. (not visit • Amish)
3. If Joshua didn't have a microwave, ______. (eat • cold food)
4. The Burtons would be angry if ______. (TV • not work)
5. If Amy's brother read her texts, ______. (be • very angry)
6. If Tyler lived in Boston, ______ often. (not visit • grandma)

● b) Use your own ideas to complete the sentences.

1. If my phone didn't work, _I'd take it back to the store_.
2. Sarah's friends would be surprised if ______.
3. If Bill had to wear a uniform for his job, ______.
4. Our football players would be better if ______.

8 Put a circle around the right word or words.

1. We would like Ashley even more if she doesn't talk / (didn't talk) / talked so much.
2. If I wasn't / were / would you, I would buy a new sports bag.
3. Ethan didn't be / won't be / wouldn't be so tired if he didn't text his friends all night.
4. I wouldn't spend my holidays on a campsite if I won't / would be / were a rich sports star.

9 What's that in German?

1. The girls would call Jane if they knew her phone number.

2. If the Beckers had a garden, they would grow their own vegetables.

3. If I didn't have a phone, I wouldn't speak to my friends every day.

4. Joshua wouldn't work in the café if the boss was strict.

5. Ashley wouldn't buy so many things if she didn't surf the internet.

• 10 What would you do? Write six sentences with if. You can use these ideas more than once.

If … + star, to do magic, free time, money, … + to fly, computer, to buy, fight, food, to travel, weather, to build

1. If I were able to do magic, I would fly around the world.
2. If I could do magic, I would
3. If I had lots of money,
4.
5.
6.

11 Say it in a different way.

1. Tyler isn't on the football team because he doesn't play well.
   If Tyler played well, he would be on the football team.
2. I don't watch French TV programmes because I don't speak French.
   ______
3. The girls laugh at Amy because she wears a silly uniform for work.
   ______
4. Sarah and Emma don't eat at the Burger Bar because they're vegetarians.
   ______
5. Tom doesn't take the subway because he doesn't live in a city.
   ______

12 Read the text and complete the sentences.

Ethan often gets up late. Then he doesn't have time for breakfast. He misses the school bus, so he can't see Olivia before his first class – and he can't ask her out on a date. When he sees her again, she already has a date with another boy. It's the same every time!

1. If Ethan didn't get up late, ______ breakfast.
2. If he didn't ______ , he would be able to see Olivia before his first class.
3. ______ before his first class, he ______ ask her out on a date before another boy asks her.

13 What's that in English?

1. Wenn die Schuhe nicht so teuer wären, würde Joshua sie kaufen.
   ______
2. Ashley wäre nicht so gelangweilt, wenn sie mit ihren Freunden (zusammen) wäre.
   ______
3. Wenn ich meinen Führerschein hätte, würde ich ein Auto leihen.
   ______
4. Würde Sandra so viele Gäste einladen, wenn sie kein großes Wohnzimmer hätte?
   ______
   ______

1 Put in do, does, is or are.

1. Does ______ Tyler play basketball on Sundays?
2. ______ Ruth interested in clothes and gossip?
3. ______ families in Germany celebrate Thanksgiving?
4. ______ you allowed to go camping?
5. ______ your sister eat meat?
6. ______ the stores in your town expensive?
7. ______ you like Matt's new shoes?
8. ______ there a church in this town?

2 Match the questions and answers.

1. Where does Mark live? → C
2. Does your friend play football?
3. When will the game start?
4. Are the girls watching a DVD?
5. Will you help me with this German text?
6. What did Emily do yesterday?
7. Do the Amish have modern devices?
8. Is baseball popular in the USA?

A Sure – if I can understand it!
B Oh yes, it is!
C In Boston.
D She went bowling with her friends.
E No, they don't.
F Yes, he does – if he has time.
G No, they aren't. They've gone out to a café.
H At three o'clock, I think.

● 3 Complete the sentences with the right question tag.

1. Our visitors will be here at six o'clock, won't they ______ ?
2. New York City is an awesome place, ______ ?
3. Your parents don't go bowling, ______ ?
4. Sarah wore a nice dress yesterday, ______ ?
5. You can tidy up in the kitchen, ______ ?
6. We didn't make a lot of noise last night, ______ ?
7. Bill and Jacob aren't coming to the party, ______ ?
8. Madison looks silly in her uniform, ______ ?

4 Put in the right form of the verb.

1. What would Matt do if he didn't have ______ (not have) a phone?
2. If Olivia knew the answer to the question, she ______ (tell) us.
3. If you ______ (have) 200 dollars, what would you buy?
4. The boys ______ (not be) cold if they wore their warm clothes.
5. If Mary ______ (not go) to school with Jessica, would they still be best friends?
6. If there wasn't a big game this afternoon, Joshua ______ (stay) in bed all day.

5 Questions and answers

a) Complete the questions with who or who did.

1. Who did ______ Sarah see? – She saw her parents.
2. ______ ate all the sweets? – The children ate them.
3. ______ told you about the competition? – Danny told me.
4. ______ the boys meet? – They met a teacher.
5. ______ drew this funny picture? – My brother drew it.

b) Ask questions about the underlined words.

1. Who did Emily look after? ______ – Emily looked after her sister.
2. ______ – We talked about my new job.
3. ______ – Danny had dinner with Jennifer.
4. ______ – The girls looked at the new fashion store.

6 Complete the text.

are ✓ | ask | didn't | goes | isn't | meet | met | them | Who | Why | with | wouldn't

Austin: Hi! You're not busy at the moment, are ______ you?

Grace: No – but I have to meet Amy in 20 minutes.

Austin: If you ______ have to ______ her, we could go bowling this afternoon.

Grace: ______ didn't you ______ me earlier? Now it's too late, ______ it?

Austin: I have an idea. Would it be OK if you ______ Amy tomorrow?

Grace: No, it ______. She always ______ swimming on Sundays.

Austin: ______ does she go swimming ______?

Grace: With her boyfriend Ryan.

Austin: Well, you and I could go swimming with ______ tomorrow. Ask Amy – please!

G9 R: Gegenüberstellung: Simple present – present progressive

Revision: Simple present – present progressive

Du kennst schon die Zeiten **simple present** und **present progressive**. Hier findest du noch einmal die Situationen, in denen du sie benutzen kannst und siehst, wie sie gebildet werden.

Simple present

Das **simple present** verwendest du, wenn du sagen willst, dass jemand etwas häufig oder regelmäßig tut.

Signalwörter: always, never, sometimes, often, usually, every …

Aussagen bildest du mit der Grundform des Verbs.

I **work** every day. You never **listen**.

Achtung: **He**, **she**, **it** – das **s** muss mit:
He work**s**. She talk**s**. It rain**s**. Aber: He go**es**.

Sätze mit Vollverben verneinst du mit **don't** und **doesn't**:

I **don't play** football.

Bei Fragen mit Vollverben musst du mit **do** oder **does** beginnen:

Do you **eat** fish? **Does** he **like** games?

Present progressive

Mit dem **present progressive** kannst du sagen, was jemand gerade tut oder was im Augenblick passiert.

Signalwörter: now, at the moment

Aussagen bildest du so:
am / are / is + Verb + -ing

I**'m working** at the moment. It **is raining** now.

Achtung Schreibweise: make → mak**ing**; write → writ**ing**; run → run**ning**; sit → sit**ting**

So verneinst du Sätze:
am / are / is not + Verb + -ing:

He **isn't eating** at the moment.

Bei Fragen stellst du **am / are / is** an den Satzanfang:

Are you **listening**? **Is** she **dancing**?

Simple present und present progressive kannst du auch einsetzen, um ein **Bild** zu beschreiben. Zunächst sagst du, wen oder was du siehst. Dann beschreibst du, was jemand tut.

Simple present

Du benutzt es, um zu sagen, wer oder was auf dem Bild zu sehen ist, oder in welchem Zustand etwas ist.

There is a boy in the picture.
There are a man and a woman.
She **looks** happy.
She **has** two dogs.
The weather **is** nice. It **is** warm.

Present progressive

Du benutzt es für alle Handlungen, die im Bild zu sehen sind und für alles, was jemand tut.

The boy **is riding** a mountain bike.
They**'re sitting** in camping chairs.
She**'s wearing** boots.
They **are playing** with a ball.
The sun **is shining**. It **isn't raining**.

1 Put in the correct form of the simple present.

1. California *has* (have) many popular beaches.
2. It ______________ (not rain) there very often.
3. People ______________ (spend) a lot of time outside.
4. You ______________ (not need) a ticket for the beach.

2 Complete the sentences.

am not doing	aren't watching	are talking	is doing
isn't phoning	is talking ✓		

1. Look, there's Amy. She _is talking_ to somebody.
2. The TV is on but the boys ______________ it.
3. You mustn't talk to Bill when he ______________ his homework.
4. We can go out now. I ______________ anything important.
5. Let's listen to Emma and Josh. Maybe they ______________ about us.
6. Daniel is asleep right now. He ______________ his friends.

3 Put in the correct form of the present progressive.

1. Right now Ashley _is planning_ (plan) her holiday.
2. She ______________ (not sit) in her room.
3. The boys ______________ (play) football with friends.
4. Look at Jacob and Mario! They ______________ (not run) very fast.
5. Matt ______________ (make) a cake for his mum's birthday.
6. His parents ______________ (not have) a party today.

4 Find the signal words.

a) Put a circle around the signal words.

Matt is phoning his girlfriend Sarah right now. He always calls her at the same time every evening. Sarah is watching a video at the moment. She can do two or three things at the same time. She sometimes calls friends while she's doing her homework. Matt usually knows when Sarah isn't listening to him. But he never asks, "Sarah, what are you doing now?" He doesn't say anything until Sarah asks, "Matt, are you still there?"

b) Write the signal words in the correct box.

simple present	present progressive
______________	now
______________	______________
______________	______________
______________	______________
______________	______________

5 Put a circle around the correct form.

1. Do you listen / Are you listening / You listening to music at the moment?
2. Emma never forgets / doesn't never forget / is never forgetting her phone.
3. I do often play / am often playing / often play baseball.
4. Every morning our neighbor walks / is walking / does walk past our house.
5. I like that new jacket. It is looking / looks / looking really cool.
6. Look at that boy over there. He doesn't carry / is carrying / carries a very big backpack.

6 Complete the sentences.

are playing | enjoys | goes | have | is enjoying | is staying ✓ | look | sits | walks

1. Right now, Jessica is staying ______ with friends near Los Angeles.
2. She always ______ her visits to California.
3. Her friends ______ a nice swimming pool.
4. The weather can be very hot. Then Jessica ______ inside, or she ______ under a tree.
5. Every morning she ______ to the beach for a surfing lesson, and now she ______ ______ a swim in the sea.
6. Some people ______ volleyball on the beach right now. They ______ very happy.

7 Look at the picture. Complete the sentences.

carry | have | hold | look | sit | wear ✓

1. A girl is wearing ______ a red dress.
2. She ______ long dark hair.
3. Two men ______ backpacks.
4. A woman ______ a cat.
5. She ______ happy.
6. A boy ______ on a wall.

8 Match the questions and answers.

1. Why are you waiting here? → D
2. Where do you go in the evenings?
3. What is Joshua cooking for dinner?
4. Do the Baxters often eat in restaurants?
5. Where is Emily going?
6. Why do you spend your holidays in California?

A Because the weather is usually very good.
B To the Sunny Café. She works there.
C No, they don't. They like cooking at home.
D Because Tyler's flight will arrive in 20 minutes.
E No idea, but it smells great!
F To the sports club usually, but sometimes to the cinema.

9 Simple present or present progressive?

a) Put in the right form of the verb.

1. Sandy often *writes* ________ (write) to her friends back in the Midwest.
2. Right now she ________ (read) a message from Becky.
3. At the moment the sun ________ (not shine).
4. Sandy sometimes ________ (miss) her old life in the Midwest.
5. But she ________ usually ________ (not have) any problems with her new life in California.
6. Now Becky and her parents ________ (plan) a trip to California in the summer.

● b) Complete the sentences. Put the verbs in the right form.

be | have ✓ | look | sit | not rain | wear

Becky *has* ________ a nice photo of Sandy's house in California. Sandy's sisters ________ by the swimming pool. They ________ sunglasses. There ________ some plants around the swimming pool, but they ________ very dry. It ________ at the moment.

10 What's that in German?

1. At the moment Ethan isn't phoning his friends.

____

2. We never spend our holidays in California.

____

3. This ad doesn't look very clear.

____

4. What are you reading on the internet?

____

11 Write the dialogue.

What • you • do • right now?	Bill:	*What are you doing right now?*
watch • a surf video	Ryan:	______
have lessons • every weekend		______
you • like • all water sports?	Bill:	______
I • not like • canoeing	Ryan:	______
I • sit • next to swimming pool	Bill:	______
		______ It's really the best place to be.
it • be • great	Ryan:	Yeah, ______
I • come		Wait for me. – ______

12 Put in the correct verb forms.

It's Friday evening. Tyler *is watching* (watch) a video on his phone. His brother Will ______ (listen) to music.

Tyler: Hey Will, come and watch this! A guy ______ (surf) in a storm.

Will: You know I ______ (not like) surfing. And I'______ (wait) for a call from Ashley at the moment.

Tyler: Just come here for a moment. Look! That guy ______ (have) the most fantastic equipment! He ______ (look) so cool! I'______ (save) all my money now for equipment like that.

Will: How often ______ (you – go) surfing? Once a year? You can hire equipment quite cheaply. – Oh, that's my phone. Hi Ashley! … Right now? I'______ (talk) to Tyler. … ______ (you – have) time for a movie? … Great!

Now Will ______ (put on) his jacket. Tyler ______ (watch) the video. He often ______ (dream) about his future as a successful surfer.

13 What's that in English?

1. Was machst du gerade? ______
2. Wie oft sieht Tanya jede Woche fern? ______
3. Diese Anzeige sieht nicht sehr ansprechend aus. ______
4. Schau mal! Die Frau rennt weg! ______

G10 R: Adjektive und Adverbien

Revision: Adjectives and adverbs

Ein **Adjektiv** (Eigenschaftswort) beschreibt eine Person oder eine Sache.

Sandra is a **good** surfer.	Sandra ist eine gute Surferin.
A helicopter tour is **fantastic**.	Ein Hubschrauberflug ist fantastisch.

Ein **Adverb** beschreibt, wie jemand etwas tut oder wie etwas geschieht.
Man erkennt Adverbien durch ein angehängtes **-ly**.

Look, she is running **slowly**.	Schau, sie läuft langsam.
It happened **quickly**.	Es geschah schnell.

Achtung Schreibweise: happy – happ**ily**; careful – careful**ly**, comfortable – comfortab**ly**, fantastic – fantastic**ally**

Es gibt Adverbien, die sich nicht verändern:

Basketball is a **fast** game.	(Adjektiv)	Basketball ist ein schnelles Spiel.
Look, the players are running **fast**.	(Adverb)	Schau, die Spieler rennen schnell.
That was a **hard** exercise.	(Adjektiv)	Das war eine schwierige Übung.
Tom has to work **hard** every day.	(Adverb)	Tom muss jeden Tag schwer arbeiten.

Es gibt auch unregelmäßige Adverbien:

This is a **good** surfboard.	(Adjektiv)	Das ist ein gutes Surfbrett.
I can surf very **well** with it.	(Adverb)	Ich kann sehr gut damit surfen.

Achtung Ausnahme! Manche Verben drücken **keine** Tätigkeit aus, z. B. **look**, **feel**, **seem**, **sound**.
Nach diesen Verben verwendest du ein **Adjektiv**:

I **feel** so **sad**.	Ich fühle mich so traurig.
You **look happy** today.	Du siehst heute glücklich aus.
This exercise **seems easy**.	Diese Aufgabe scheint leicht zu sein.
That **sounds good**.	Das klingt gut.

1 Make the adjectives into adverbs.

1. clear	clearly	9. different	
2. exciting		10. sad	
3. nervous		11. serious	
4. secret		12. cheeky	
5. cute		13. successful	
6. scary		14. busy	
7. awful		15. lazy	
8. crazy		16. furious	

2 Complete the sentences. Use the present progressive and make adverbs.

awful | careful | happy | nervous | proud | quick ✓

1. run

2. work

3. wait

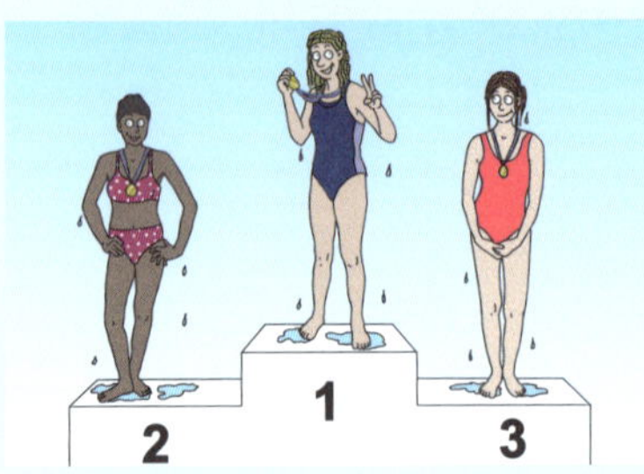

4. stand

5. sing

6. climb

1. The woman _is running quickly_ .
2. The man ______________________ .
3. The boy ______________________ .
4. The girls ______________________ .
5. The children ______________________ .
6. The friends ______________________ .

3 Put a circle around the correct form.

1. Joshua is talking excited / (excitedly) / excitedily to his friends.
2. This new ad for California is catchily / catchfully / catchy.
3. I'm waiting patient / patiently / patientely for a text message from Susan.
4. Look. – Madison is sitting lazy / lazily / lazylly by the swimming pool.
5. The Burtons walked safely / safly / safe home along the dark road.
6. Tyler secret / secretally / secretly told Ashley about his brother's plans.
7. On a clearly / clear / clearily day you can see the mountains from here.
8. Can you play the guitar? – Yes, but I play very badly / bad / worst.

4 Adjective or adverb? Complete the sentences.

1. Jessica is very _proud_ ______ (proud) of her new mountain bike.
2. If she rides her bike ______________ (crazy), she'll have an accident.
3. They don't go to the beach when the weather is ______________ (awful).
4. William is ______________ (patient) explaining his new phone to his parents.
5. His mom always listens ______________ (careful); then she asks lots of questions.
6. Amy had an ______________ (exciting) plane trip yesterday.
7. Her plane had to fly through a storm, but it landed ______________ (safe).

5 Complete the sentences.

scary | fast | happily | hard | heavy | sadly | secret | well ✓

1. The children like music, but they don't sing _well_ ______ .
2. Can you help me with this box? It's very ______________ .
3. If I work ______________ , maybe I'll win a prize.
4. It was the worst day of Tom's life. He said goodbye to Sarah and walked ______________ home.
5. Is your car slow? – No, it isn't. It goes really ______________ .
6. I don't usually like ______________ movies, but *The Ancient Forest* was great!
7. What is Madison doing? – She's talking ______________ to Tyler.
8. They have ______________ plans for a trip to Hollywood.

● 6 Say it in a different way.

a) Use adjectives.

1. Julia swims well.	_She's a good swimmer_ ______ .
2. Emma works hard.	She is ______________ .
3. Joshua planned his trip carefully.	He made ______________ for his trip.
4. Jack surfs fantastically.	______________ .

b) Use adverbs.

1. Mrs Benson has a loud voice.	_She talks loudly_ ______ .
2. There was a nervous shout.	Somebody ______________ .
3. Matt is a fast player.	______________ .
4. Amy has a job in a busy office.	People ______________ there.

7 Put a circle around the correct word.

1. Movie actor Samantha always looks very relaxed / relaxedly.
2. But in fact she often feels nervous / nervously when she is waiting patient / patiently for reporters.
3. In TV interviews people ask her excited / excitedly about her plans for the future.
4. Samantha sounds very excited / excitedly about her ideas for new movies.
5. In the future she wants to act different / differently.
6. "Next year I'm going to play the part of a woman who seems very happy / happily.
7. But in fact this woman worries serious / seriously about everything.
8. It's a very interesting / interestingly part," Samantha says.
9. She certainly sounds confident / confidently about her career in Hollywood!

8 Complete the sentences. Look at the pictures.

angry | careful | comfortable | hard | hungry | interesting ✓

1. This book sounds interesting __________ .
2. He's sitting ____________________ .
3. She looks ______________ .
4. Please carry those boxes ____________________ !
5. She's working ______________ .
6. He feels ______________ .

9 Adjective or adverb? Complete the text. Do not use the same word more than once.

beautiful | busy | exciting | famous | happy | hard | interesting | lazy

In the summer many people in California live ____________ on the beach. Or they work ____________ at their favorite sport. In San Francisco you can take an ____________ ride on a cable car and visit the ____________ harbor. If you go to Los Angeles, why not visit Hollywood? There you can feel ____________ like a movie star!

10 What's that in English?

1. Max muss die Küche aufräumen. Das ist harte Arbeit.

   ____

2. Sarah kann sehr gut Gitarre spielen.

   ____

3. Der neue Kinofilm klingt spannend.

   ____

4. Wir werden den Weg zum Strand leicht finden.

   ____

5. Ich fühle mich oft sehr müde.

   ____

6. Die Freunde haben den Kletterkurs erfolgreich beendet.

   ____

   ____

11 Complete the text with the correct forms.

Emily *suddenly* (sudden) saw an ad for a climbing trip.

"This looks ____________ (exciting)!" she thought. "I can't climb very ____________ (good), but I'd like to learn together with other people."

She started the trip ____________ (happy) on Friday morning. The first two days were ____________ (hard) work, and everyone fell asleep very ____________ (quick) in the evening. But after that Emily climbed the high rocks ____________ (easy), even the ones that looked ____________ (difficult) at first. At the end of the trip Emily felt very ____________ (confident).

"I'm going to take climbing ____________ (serious)," she said.

G11 R: Das Perfekt

Revision: The present perfect

Wenn eine Handlung in der Vergangenheit beginnt und in der Gegenwart zu einem Ergebnis führt, verwendest du das **present perfect**:
have/has + 3. Form des Verbs (past participle).
Bei den meisten Verben hängst du ein **-ed** an das Verb: help → help**ed**

Signalwörter	
already	schon
just	gerade
not … yet	noch … nicht
never	noch nie
ever (in Fragen)	jemals (in Fragen)
since	seit (Zeitpunkt)
for	seit (Zeitspanne)

Eine Liste der unregelmäßigen Verben findest du auf Seite 79.

Einige Verben haben unregelmäßige 3. Formen: z. B. be → **been**; write → **written**

I **have** just **posted** a photo. — Ich habe gerade ein Foto verschickt.
She **has** already **written** ten text messages. — Sie hat schon zehn SMS geschrieben.

Um Sätze zu verneinen, benutzt du **haven't** oder **hasn't** (bei he, she, it):

I **haven't been** to California yet. — Ich bin noch nicht in Kalifornien gewesen.
She **hasn't seen** Los Angeles yet. — Sie hat Los Angeles noch nicht gesehen.

Fragen und Kurzantworten bildest du so:

Have you ever **been** to San Francisco?	Yes, I **have**.	No, I **haven't**.
Has your sister ever **met** a famous star?	Yes, she **has**.	No, she **hasn't**.

Present perfect mit **for** und **since**
since (**seit**) verwendest du vor einem **Zeitpunkt**, z. B. **since** 5 o'clock, **since** July, **since** 2013.
for (**seit**) verwendest du vor einer **Zeitspanne**, z. B. **for** five hours, **for** three years, **for** a long time.

I haven't seen Lara **since** Monday. — Ich habe Lara **seit** Montag nicht gesehen.
I haven't seen Lara **for** a week. — Ich habe Lara **seit** einer Woche nicht gesehen.

Wie im Präsens gibt es im Perfekt eine Verlaufsform (**present perfect progressive**).
Damit betonst du die Dauer der Handlung. Vergleiche:

I **have been living** in Los Angeles **for** two years. — Ich **lebe seit** zwei Jahren in Los Angeles.

1 Complete the table.

infinitive	simple past	past participle
1. look	looked	looked
2. speak		
3. have		
4. do		

2 Put the verbs in the present perfect.

1. Dan has never taken (take) a ride on a cable car.
2. The Leroys ______ (be) on the beach for a long time.
3. Madison ______ (find) a new job in San Francisco.
4. Most visitors to Hollywood ______ (see) the Walk of Fame.
5. My sister isn't here. She ______ (go) to the sports store.
6. I ______ (have) enough sports for one day. Let's go home.
7. This is Ed. He ______ (come) to stay with us.
8. Sarah ______ (post) more photos of her friends.

3 Put a circle around the signal words for the present perfect.

Tyler has just come back from a short trip to California. He hasn't put away his things yet, but he has already called Jessica. He always phones her every evening. – He has never forgotten. But Tyler hasn't seen her since last week. He and Jessica have been friends for five months.

"I went to see the Hall of Fame on Friday," he tells her. "It was fantastic. Have you ever been to Hollywood?"

"No, I haven't had the chance yet," she tells him. "Maybe we can go there together next year."

4 Write questions and answers.

a) Complete the questions and write short answers.

1. Has Amy read Emma's blog? (read) – No, she hasn't.
2. ______ you ______ a new smartphone? (buy) – No, ______.
3. ______ surfing ______ popular in your country? (become) – Yes, ______.
4. ______ I ______ you about my website? (tell) – No, ______.

● b) Make questions and answers.

1. What • you • just • find? – Tutorial video • surfing
   What have you just found? – I've just found a tutorial video about surfing.
2. Where • Hannah • be? • just • a café • near beach
   ______
3. Martin • already • buy • new clothes? – No, • new guitar
   ______
4. Why • you • not answer • texts yet? – Because • not have • time
   ______

5 Write what they have or haven't done.

break | build ✓ | buy | lose | hurt | write

1. The workers have built a bridge. They haven't built a skyscraper ______ .
2. Emily ______ .
3. Matt ______ .
4. We ______ .
5. I ______ .
6. My sister ______ .

6 Complete the dialogue.

Amy: Have you had ______ (you – have) breakfast yet?

Emily: No, ______ , but I ______ (already – make) some tea.

Amy: Great! Jacob ______ (just – send) us a message.

Emily: Really? I ______ (not read) it yet.

Amy: Jacob says he ______ (just – meet) Tyler.

Emily: Tyler! I ______ (not see) him for weeks! ______ (Jacob and Tyler – make) any plans for today?

Amy: No idea. I ______ (just – send) Jacob a text to ask him, but he ______ (not answer) yet.

Emily: OK, let's have breakfast while we're waiting. I can see that you ______ (buy) my favorite food!

7 Put in for or since.

1. We haven't heard from Sarah for ______ three days.
2. Have you seen Marco ______ his birthday?
3. Daniel hasn't stopped talking ______ twenty minutes.
4. Hannah and Olivia have been friends ______ years.
5. Michael has had a smartphone ______ January.
6. My brother hasn't bought a CD ______ he left school.

8 Match the questions and answers.

1. Where did Samantha buy her guitar?
2. Did Josh post anything new on his blog last week?
3. How long have the kids lived in California?
4. Have you read Daniel's new blog?
5. Why did the Robsons move away from Los Angeles?
6. Has Hannah just bought a new guitar?

A No, not yet. I haven't had time to read any long texts.
B Yes, she has. She found it on the internet.
C They didn't like the city. And then their mum got a job in Texas.
D She bought it on the internet.
E Yes, he posted a text about his trip to Los Angeles.
F About five years, I think. They love it here!

● 9 Simple past or present perfect?

a) Put a circle around the signal words for the simple past. Underline those for the present perfect.

b) Put in the correct verb forms.

1. Madison took ______ (take) some cool photos at a concert last week but she hasn't sent ______ (not send) them to her friends yet.
   She ______ (never have) her own blog, but she ______ (start) posting photos on social media sites last year when she ______ (be) 14.
2. William ______ (not have) a radio for two years now.
   He ______ (sell) it on the internet in March when he ______ (get) his first smartphone.
3. Last weekend Ryan ______ (have) an awful surprise when he ______ (check) his messages. Some people from his school ______ (be) very unfriendly to him. He ______ (already tell) his parents about the messages.
   They ______ (be) worried about cyberbullying, but it ______ (not happen) again yet.

10 What's that in German?

1. Matt hasn't read his messages yet.

____

2. Emily has just come home.

____

3. Have you ever bought a pet on the internet?

____

4. I haven't seen my friends for two days.

____

5. The children have never swum in the sea.

____

6. Ashley has already posted twenty photos.

____

11 Find the right order. Number the sentences 1 – 10.

Tom		Sarah	
A magazine? Do you still read magazines in your family? We gave them up years ago.	☐	Yes, it's good. Last week they had special offers on girls' shoes. I didn't look at the boys' shoes.	☐
No, I guess boys' shoes aren't your thing. Maybe I'll go down to the store. Do you want to come with me?	☐	Yes, I have. My mom asked me to buy some food for dinner and a magazine.	☐
I'd like some new shoes too. Is that store good? I've never been there.	☐	Yes, they are. I buy most of my clothes on the internet. But these shoes I'm wearing came from the new store downtown.	☐
Hi, Sarah! Have you just been shopping?	1	Sorry, I can't come. Mom is waiting for these things.	☐
Do you? Well, well! But there are so many fashion websites. And I guess the clothes are cheaper online.	☐	Well, I haven't bought a magazine for myself for a long time. But I sometimes have a look at Mom's fashion magazines.	☐

12 Write the interview.

Reporter	Ryan
1. When • you • join • social media site?	1. 13
2. cyberbullying • ever • happen • to you?	2. never • have • awful messages
3. How long • you • have • blog?	3. for two years • start • become • sports fan
4. you • find • many fans • yet?	4. yes • hundreds • already • read • blog

1. Reporter: *When did you join a social media site?*
   Ryan: ______________________
2. Reporter: ______________________
   Ryan: ______________________
3. Reporter: ______________________
   Ryan: ______________________
4. Reporter: ______________________
   Ryan: ______________________

13 What's that in English?

1. Warum sind soziale Medien so beliebt geworden?
   ____
2. Hast du jemals ein Computerspiel erfunden?
   ____
3. Letzte Woche hat Emma einen Blogger im echten Leben kennen gelernt.
   ____
4. Ich habe noch kein gutes Tutorial fürs Surfen gefunden.
   ____

14 Simple past or present perfect? Put in the correct form of the verbs.

Social media *have been* (be) with us for many years now. It all ______________ (start) with the internet in the 1990s. Then mobile devices ______________ (become) popular very quickly.

In fact, last year only two of my friends still ______________ (have) an old-fashioned telephone at home! Many people ______________ (already throw out) their maps, their radios, their telephone books. Today, smartphones ______________ (replace) them.

1 Match the questions and answers.

1. When do you usually have breakfast?
2. Is Ashley working in her room?
3. Have you ever been to San Francisco?
4. When did you check your e-mails yesterday?
5. What has Sarah just bought?
6. Are you having dinner?

A Yes, I have. My mum took me there last March.
B Not at the moment. I never eat when I'm online.
C At seven. But yesterday I got up very late.
D A new phone. She lost her old one on Saturday.
E At seven. But there wasn't any message from my boss.
F No, she's just gone out to the supermarket.

2 Write down what they are doing or what they have done.

break | buy | read | take ✓ | win | write

1. Jack *is taking photos of a/his cat* ______.
2. Susan ______.
3. Julia ______.
4. The boys ______.
5. Luke ______.
6. Somebody ______.

3 Write the signal words in the correct box.

already | an hour ago | ever | every day ✓ | not … yet | now | often | usually | yesterday | at the moment

simple present	present progressive	simple past	present perfect
every day			

4 Complete the sentences.

furious | furiously | proud | proudly | strict | strictly ✓

1. After the problems with cyberbullying, Mrs Leroy spoke very _strictly_ ________ to all her students.
2. Matt looked at his brother ________ when he saw the broken chair.
3. At that moment Tyler felt very ________ of his team.
4. Don't worry about our English teacher. He sounds very ________ , but he's OK.
5. Don't post those photos of Ryan! He'll be ________ if he sees them.
6. Louisa ________ showed her new phone to the whole class.

5 Complete the dialogue.

Michael: Hi Linda! _Have you finished_ ________ (you – finish) your History homework yet?

Linda: No, I ________ . I ________ (check) the internet yesterday and I ________ (write) my text right now.

Michael: Where ________ (you – usually – do) your homework?

Linda: In my room. But at the moment I ________ (sit) on the beach.

Michael: Cool! ________ (you – already – meet) any friends there?

Linda: No, not yet. But I ________ (call) Matt and Amy a few minutes ago. They ________ (pack) a picnic for all of us right now.

Michael: That ________ (sound) great! I'm on my way too.

6 Complete the text.

actually | ago | awful | changed | exciting | got | happily | has ✓ | have | made | quickly | started | successful | yet

California _has_ ________ always been the place for new ideas and ________ inventions. People there first ________ using the internet about 30 years ________ , and since then social media and mobile devices have ________ our lives.

Matt ________ his first smartphone for his thirteenth birthday. Since then he has ________ hundreds of friends through the social media. But he hasn't met all of them ________ .

"Well, ________ , I don't always need to be together with people," he says. "I can sit ________ with my smartphone for hours. I often find ________ new music videos or tutorials. And if my friends ________ sent me texts, I always write back ________ . Life without my smartphone would be ________ !"

G12 Das Passiv

Passive voice (simple present and simple past)

Mit dem Passiv kannst du über eine Handlung Auskunft geben, ohne zu sagen, wer die Handlung ausführt. Im Vordergrund steht die Handlung.

So bildest du das **Passiv** im **simple present: am / are / is + 3. Form des Verbs** (past participle)

English **is spoken** in a lot of countries.	Englisch **wird** in vielen Ländern **gesprochen**.
Discrimination **isn't accepted**.	Diskriminierung **wird nicht akzeptiert**.
Spices and flour **are mixed**.	Gewürze und Mehl **werden gemischt**.

So bildest du das Passiv im **simple past: was / were + 3. Form des Verbs** (past participle)

The city of Atlanta **was founded** by Indians.	Atlanta **wurde** von Indianern **gegründet**.
The highest building in Atlanta **wasn't finished** until 1993.	Das höchste Gebäude in Atlanta **wurde nicht** vor 1993 **fertiggestellt**.
New streets **were built** in the city.	Neue Straßen **wurden** in der Stadt **gebaut**.

Willst du in einem Passivsatz sagen, **wer** die Handlung ausführt, ergänzt du ihn oder sie mit **by**.

Atlanta **was called** 'Standing Peachtree' **by** the Indians.	Atlanta **wurde von** den Indianern „Standing Peachtree" **genannt**.
New dishes **were brought** here **by** the immigrants.	Neue Gerichte **wurden von** den Einwanderern hierher **gebracht**.

1 Put the words in the right order.

1. made • eggs • This dish • is • with

   This dish is made with eggs.

2. most countries • are • Vegetables • in • grown

   ____

3. all over • spoken • English • is • the world

   ____

4. in Germany • not • celebrated • Thanksgiving • is

   ____

5. checked • every week • are • The school buses

   ____

6. online • booked • Most tickets • are

   ____

2 Complete the sentences. Use the passive voice (simple present).

1. New houses _are built_ (build) here every year.
2. The streets ______________________ (not clean) every day.
3. Sometimes plants ______________________ (steal) from the park.
4. The new music store ______________________ (call) 'The coolest place in the South'.
5. Every year the winner of the music competition ______________________ (choose) in June.
6. This dish ______________________ (not eat) with a knife and fork. You use your fingers.
7. Our visitors ______________________ (expect) at 7:30 p.m.
8. Some of the best inventions ______________________ (not plan). They just happen!

3 Complete the sentences. Look at the pictures and say how this dish is cooked.

put in | cook | cut ✓ | eat | fry | mix

1. Vegetables _are cut_ into pieces.
2. They ______________________ in oil.
3. Spices ______________________ .
4. Tomato juice ______________________ with the vegetables.
5. The vegetables ______________________ for 20 minutes.
6. This dish ______________________ with rice.

4 Put a circle around the correct form.

1. Too much food has thrown / (is thrown) away.
2. Vegetables are served / is served with rice or potatoes.
3. The new law is explained / are explained on many websites.
4. Machines have repaired / are repaired in this workshop.

5 Make passive sentences. Begin with the underlined words.

1. People organize exciting holidays in the South.
   Exciting holidays are organized in the South.
2. They book places on campsites and in hotels.
3. Tourists enjoy meals in restaurants and cafés.
4. They don't buy food online.
5. People speak Spanish in some places.
6. They use English as the first language.
7. TV companies show programs in the two languages.
8. People don't read newspapers every day.

6 What's that in German?

1. Tomatoes are grown in Florida.
2. French is spoken in parts of Canada.
3. Some German dishes are cooked in American restaurants.
4. A lot of photos are taken at the music festivals in New Orleans.
5. African Americans are not always respected.
6. German isn't taught at all American schools.

7 Write down what is done. Use the notes.

1. the football game • not show • on TV
   The football game isn't shown on TV.
2. sometimes • people • attack • in the park
   ____
3. a special meal • cook • for the children
   ____
4. the French text • translate • for Americans
   ____
5. the tickets • not book • online
   ____
6. chocolates • buy • for the stars
   ____
7. during the carnival southern food • sell • in the streets
   ____
8. lots of Spanish words • use • in American English
   ____

8 Complete the text.

Southern Sweet Tea

add · keep · make ✓ · mix · put · take · serve

1. Southern Sweet Tea is made ______ with hot water, tea bags, sugar and ice.
2. The tea bags ______________ into the hot water.
3. After 5 – 10 minutes the tea bags ______________ out.
4. Sugar ______________ , and then it ______________ with the tea.
5. When the tea is cold, it ______________ in tall glasses with ice.
6. The tea ______________ in the fridge.

9 Complete the sentences. Use the passive voice (simple past).

1. Last week a picture was stolen (steal) from a house in town.
2. The picture ______ (own) by a famous movie star.
3. Two computers ______ (take) too.
4. No sounds ______ (hear) by the people in the house.
5. Yesterday police officers ______ (call) to a campsite.
6. Some cars and caravans ______ (search).
7. The picture ______ (find) in an old car.
8. The driver of the car ______ (arrest).
9. The happy movie star ______ (interview) by a reporter.
10. A photo ______ (post) on the movie star's website.

● 10 Make passive sentences.

1. Somebody attacked a girl in the street yesterday evening.
   A girl was attacked in the street yesterday evening.
2. The person pushed her against the wall.
   ______
3. Then the person took the girl's bag and phone.
   ______
4. But the person didn't hurt her badly.
   ______
5. Later two teenagers found her on the ground.
   ______ on the ground.
6. An ambulance took the girl to a hospital.
   ______
7. A doctor put bandages on her hand and her leg.
   ______
8. Then the doctor sent her home in a taxi.
   ______

● 11 What's that in English?

1. Diskriminierung wird von den meisten Leuten nicht toleriert.

____

2. Touristen werden durch die berühmten Musikfeste angezogen.

____

3. Dieses Gericht wird mit einem Löffel gegessen.

____

4. Dieses afrikanische Restaurant wurde vor 40 Jahren eröffnet.

____

5. Die alten Häuser wurden letztes Jahr verkauft.

____

6. Diese Maschine wurde nicht von deutschen Einwanderern erfunden.

____

● 12 Complete the text about the city of Baton Rouge in Louisiana.

Baton Rouge is a city on the Mississippi River with about 230,000 inhabitants. The land *was called* (call) 'Istrouma' by the Native Americans who lived here, before their land _______________ (take) by Europeans. In the 17th century some places in Louisiana _______________ (settle) by the French. Then the region _______________ (take) by the Spanish.

In 1803 the land _______________ (sell) to the USA.

In 1849 Baton Rouge _______________ (choose) as the capital of Louisiana.

From 1861 to 1865 terrible battles _______________ (fight) in Louisiana and in other states.

In 1906 oil and gas _______________ (find). This _______________ (call) 'the black gold rush'.

Industries _______________ (plan) and factories _______________ (build).

Today Baton Rouge _______________ (know) for its successful high-tech companies.

G13 Indirekte Rede (ohne Zeitverschiebung)

Reported speech (without backshift)

Mit der indirekten Rede kannst du über das berichten, was jemand anderes **gerade gesagt hat**. Du beginnst mit **He says that . . . / She says that . . .** usw. Das Wort **that** kann man auch weglassen.

Positive Aussagen und verneinte Sätze in der indirekten Rede bildest du so:

Direkte Rede	Indirekte Rede
Anna says, "**I like** Florida."	Anna says (that) **she likes** Florida.
Anna says, "**We want** to see the alligators."	Anna says (that) **they want** to see the alligators.
Anna says, "**I don't need** a hotel."	Anna says (that) **she doesn't need** a hotel.

Beachte die Änderungen:

I	→ **he/she**	**my**	→ **his/her**
we	→ **they**	**our**	→ **their**
(I) **like**	→ (he/she) **likes**		
(I) **don't** . . .	→ (he/she) **doesn't** . . .		

Fragen in der indirekten Rede werden so wiedergegeben:
Du beginnst z. B. mit **She asks if . . .** Sie fragt, **ob** . . .
Bei Fragen mit Fragewörtern beginnst du z. B. mit **He asks where . . .** Er fragt, **wo/wohin** . . .

Direkte Rede	Indirekte Rede
Anna asks Ethan, "**Do you like** alligators?"	She asks Ethan **if he likes** alligators.
Nick asks, "**Where do you go** camping?"	He asks **where they go** camping.

Erkenne die Zeitform in der **Frage** der direkten Rede (hier: **simple present**) und bilde in der indirekten Rede einen **Satz** im **simple present** nach der Regel **S**ubjekt – **V**erb – **O**bjekt!

1 Report what they say.

1. Noah says, "I don't have a brother."
   Noah says that *he doesn't have a brother* .
2. Anna says, " My phone is broken."
   Anna says that ______ .
3. Ashley says, "We're watching the race."
   Ashley says that ______ .
4. Tyler says, "My parents don't go fishing."
   Tyler says that ______ .
5. Emily says, "I'm not interested in bird watching."
   Emily says that ______ .
6. Jacob says, "I can't find my ticket."
   Jacob says that ______ .

2 Report the questions.

1. A girl: Matt, do you go swimming with your friends?
   She asks Matt if he goes swimming with his friends ____________.
2. A boy: Ryan, is your dad staying at a hotel?
   He asks Ryan ____________.
3. A boy: Emma, do you like my new shoes?
   He asks Emma ____________.
4. A girl: Michael, can you lend me your phone?
   She asks Michael ____________.
5. A boy: Joshua, does Tyler call his friends every day?
   He asks Joshua ____________.
6. A girl: Mom, can we have our party in the living room?
   She asks ____________.

3 Report the questions.

1. They want to know what Brad's name is ____________.
2. They ask (him) ____________.
3. They want to know ____________.
4. They ask (him) ____________.
5. They want to know ____________.
6. They ask (him) ____________.

4 Report what Sarah says on her website.

I like	I don't like
my friends camping snakes	our town my sister's music vegetables

Sarah says that she likes her friends and camping ____________.

She says ____________.

Sarah says that ____________

____________ or ____________.

She says ____________.

5 Report the dialogue.

1. Emily: Do you like sports?
   Emily asks Julia *if she likes sports* ________________ .
2. Julia: I don't like sports, but all my friends love it.
   Julia says that ________________ .
3. Emily: What is your favorite hobby?
   Emily wants to know ________________ .
4. Julia: I play music in my free time.
   Julia says that ________________ .
5. Emily: My friends and I want to start our own band.
   Emily says that she and ________________ .
6. Julia: Oh, can I join you?
   Julia asks ________________ .

6 Match the questions and answers.

1. Julie asks Michael if he likes climbing. → C
2. Michael wants to know where Julie goes at the weekend.
3. Amy asks Madison why she doesn't like climbing.
4. Madison wants to know if Amy watches NASCAR races.
5. Tyler wants to know where Ryan goes climbing.
6. Ryan asks Madison if she is enjoying her trip.

A "Yes, I do, if I have a ticket."
B "Of course! It's great here!"
C "No, I don't. I think it's boring."
D "In California."
E "I don't find it exciting."
F "To the beach or maybe to the sports club."

7 Write the dialogue.

1. Emma tells Jack she wants to talk to him.	*"I want to talk to you."*
2. Jack says he is having his breakfast.	________________
3. Emma tells Jack that she always drinks milk for breakfast.	________________
4. Jack tells her he doesn't like milk. His mum always makes tea for him.	________________
5. Emma tells him he is old enough to make his own tea.	________________

G14 Indirekte Rede (mit Zeitverschiebung)

Reported speech (with backshift)

Mit der indirekten Rede kannst du über etwas berichten, was jemand **vor einiger Zeit gesagt hat**. Du beginnst mit **He said that ... / She told me that ...** usw. Das Wort **that** kann man auch weglassen. Das Verb des Satzes wird vom **simple present** in das **simple past** zurückgesetzt. Das nennt man **backshift**.
Backshift gilt auch für die Verneinung: aus **don't / doesn't** wird **didn't**.

Positive Aussagen und verneinte Sätze in der indirekten Rede bildest du so:

Direkte Rede	Indirekte Rede
Al Lane said, "I **get up** at 6 a.m."	Al Lane told me (that) he **got up** at 6 a.m.
He said, "There **are** 20 alligators."	He said (that) there **were** 20 alligators.
He said, "We **don't get** a lot of visitors."	He said (that) they **didn't get** a lot of visitors.

1 Report what Jacob said.

1. "William plays the guitar."
   Jacob said that William *played the guitar*.
2. "I don't know much about music."
   Jacob told his friends that ______.
3. "My sisters often watch music videos."
   Jacob said that ______.
4. "I'm very good at tennis."
   He told us that ______.
5. "There are two sports clubs in town."
   He said that ______.
6. "We don't talk about football in my family."
   Jacob told Ryan that ______.
7. "My father often goes out on the river in his free time, and I sometimes go with him."
   Jacob said that ______
   ______ and that ______.
8. "We never catch any fish, so we have to buy some for our dinner."
   He told me that ______
   ______.

2 Report what Emily said.

a) Put a circle around the words which you must change in reported speech.

My friends don't make music. But they listen to bands and singers. We sometimes go to concerts together, but I don't buy expensive tickets. I prefer to download music. My sister listens to it with me in our room.

b) Report what she said.

Emily said that *her friends didn't make music* ________ . But she told us that ________ . She said that ________ ________ . She told me ________ ________ . She said ________ ________ .

3 Report what Joshua said.

Daytona is very popular with all my friends: We love cars and races! But we don't often get tickets for the big race. I always look at the websites but usually the tickets are too expensive for us. We watch the race on the internet, but a video doesn't feel like the real event to me.

1. Joshua said that Daytona *was very popular with all his friends* ________ .
2. He said that ________ .
3. But he told us ________ .
4. He said ________ ________ .
5. He told us that ________ ________ .

4 What did they actually say?

1. She said she didn't like snakes.	*"I don't like snakes."*
2. He said he was watching TV.	
3. She said her friend didn't eat meat.	
4. He said his friend had a brother.	

5 Report the questions the reporter asked Liam.

1. "Tell me, Liam, do you like the South?"
   She asked Liam if he liked the South ______.
2. "Are your parents from Florida?"
   She wanted to know ______.
3. "Do your friends come to your concerts?"
   She asked him ______.
4. "Is your website popular with your fans?"
   She wanted to know ______.
5. "Are you making plans for a new concert tour?"
   She wanted to know ______.
6. "Does your boss always book the hotels?"
   She asked him ______.

6 Report the questions.

1. A girl asked the woman why her restaurant was so famous ______.
2. A boy wanted to know ______.
3. A girl wanted to know ______.
4. A boy asked her ______.
5. A boy wanted to know ______.
6. A girl wanted to know ______.

7 Read Matt's notes on his interview with Ashley. Then complete his report.

my questions	Ashley's answers
1. Where – work?	wildlife center
2. enjoy – work?	yes – very much
3. When – start?	7 a.m.
4. What – do – every day?	check – animals; get – food ready
5. have – any favorite animals?	the alligators

1. Ashley told me that she worked at the wildlife center ______.
2. She said that ______.
3. She said ______.
4. I asked her what ______. She told me that ______ ______.
5. I wanted to know ______.
   She said ______.

8 English and German

a) Translate the sentences into German.

1. Amy told me she went swimming every Saturday.
   ______
2. I asked Tyler if he always spent his vacation in Florida.
   ______
3. Emily wanted to know how many brothers Matt had.
   ______
4. Sandy told me that she wasn't scared of snakes.
   ______

b) Translate the sentences into English.

1. Emma erzählte mir, dass die Tierschau immer sehr interessant ist.
   ______
2. Ryan sagte, dass er den Weg zum Strand nicht kennt.
   ______
3. Der Chef fragte uns, ob wir Karten kaufen wollen.
   ______
4. Ich wollte wissen, wann das Konzert anfängt.
   ______

9 Find the right order. Write the numbers 1 – 8.

Michael		Daniel	
Michael asked him what animals people could see at the farm.	☐	Daniel told him that it arrived at 9:30.	☐
Michael asked Daniel if he wanted to take the bus to the race too.	☐	Daniel told him that was no problem. He said that they could go to the farm together on Saturday afternoon.	☐
Michael said that he was, but he didn't have time until Saturday.	☐	Daniel said he didn't like races or cars very much. He planned to visit the animal farm during his vacation.	☐
After breakfast Michael asked Daniel when the bus to the stadium arrived at the hotel.	1	Daniel told him there were alligators, snakes and insects. He asked Michael if he was interested in a trip to the farm.	☐

● 10 Read the text. Then write the dialogue between Julie and Matt.

When Matt asked Julie what time it was, Julie said angrily that she didn't have her phone with her.
Matt wanted to know what was wrong. He asked Julie if she had a problem.
Julie answered that she had a date with Tyler at 5 p.m. and it was already 5:30. She said he wasn't usually late.
Matt asked Julie why she didn't call Tyler. Julie told Matt that he knew why. She didn't have her phone with her. Matt said that Julie could use his phone.
But Julie told him that didn't help her with her problem because she didn't have Tyler's number.

Matt: What time *is it?* ______

Julie: I don't ______

Matt: ______

Julie: ______

______

Matt: ______

Julie: ______

Matt: ______

Julie: ______

______

1 Put a circle around the correct form.

1. These sweets is made / are made / have made with sugar.
2. Our uncle is made / makes / are made his own clothes.
3. Sometimes food is bought / has bought / are bought online.
4. Our T-shirts have made / has made / are made of cotton.
5. The windows haven't cleaned / aren't cleaned / isn't cleaned every week.
6. Some friends organize / is organized / are organized parties on the beach.

2 Match the pairs.

1. Mardi Gras is celebrated every year.
2. Ashley says she wants to buy an alligator.
3. This place is often visited in winter.
4. The alligators are fed every day at 3 p.m.
5. Matt wants to know what southern fried chicken is.
6. New fast food places are opened here every year.

A Amy says they get lots of meat.
B Emma says that the best dish on the menu is usually pizza.
C Tyler says it's the best carnival in the USA.
D Joshua says, "It's fried in oil – and it's very tasty!"
E That's true. Many people think it's pretty in the snow.
F She can't. They aren't usually sold in shops or online.

3 Complete the sentences with a passive form.

a) Simple present

1. Too much food is thrown (throw) away. We must be more careful.
2. Many DVDs ______ (make) in India.
3. Porridge ______ (not eat) in my country. I don't know why it isn't popular.
4. I can understand Spanish, but it ______ (not speak) in my school.

b) Simple past

1. Last week an alligator was seen (see) in the town.
2. Two computers ______ (steal) from Joshua's house last night.
3. Some stolen goods ______ (find) in a car two days ago.
4. Amy and Emily ______ (not choose) to be cheerleaders.

4 Report what they say.

1. Madison: Do you speak English?

   Madison asks Juan if he speaks English ______.

2. Juan: Yes, I do, but I usually speak Spanish with my family.

   Juan says ______. But he says that ______ ______.

3. Madison: I think Spanish is a beautiful language.

   Madison tells Juan ______ a beautiful language.

4. Juan: Why don't you learn to speak it? I can help you.

   He asks her ______.

   He says ______.

5. Madison: That's great! We can start now with Spanish dishes.

   Madison tells him that is great. She says ______ Spanish dishes.

5 Read the dialogue. Report what they said.

Reporter: Where do you come from, Antonio?
Antonio: I come from a small town in Jamaica. My parents run a café, but they don't earn enough money for our family.
Reporter: Do you send money to your parents?
Antonio: Yes, I do. I'm the star of my football team in Florida, so I'm rich!

The reporter asked Antonio where he came from ______.

Antonio answered that ______.

He said ______ ______.

The reporter wanted to know ______.

Antonio said ______. He said ______ ______.

V

Arbeitsanweisungen Englisch – Deutsch

Ask about the underlined words.	**Frage** nach den unterstrichenen Wörtern.
Answer the questions.	**Beantworte** die Fragen.
Choose the correct word • question tag.	**Wähle** das richtige Wort • die richtige Bestätigungsfrage aus.
Compare.	**Vergleiche.**
Complete the dialogue • the sentences.	**Vervollständige** den Dialog • die Sätze.
Correct the sentences.	**Verbessere** die Sätze.
Cross out the wrong word.	**Streiche** das falsche Wort durch.
Decide if this sentence is positive, negative or a question.	**Entscheide**, ob der Satz positiv, negativ oder eine Frage ist.
Find the signal words • the right order.	**Finde** die Signalwörter • die richtige Reihenfolge.
Finish the sentences.	**Vervollständige** die Sätze.
Make sentences • questions • answers • a chain of sentences • dialogues.	**Bilde** Sätze • Fragen • Antworten • eine Satzkette • Dialoge.
Make the adjectives into adverbs.	Forme die Adjektive in Adverbien um.
Match the questions and the answers.	**Ordne** den Fragen die richtigen Antworten zu.
Match the sentences • sentence parts • the pairs.	Ordne die Sätze • Satzteile • Paare richtig zu.
You don't **need** all the words.	Du **brauchst** nicht alle Wörter.
Put in the right/correct form • the right word.	**Setze** die richtige Form • das richtige Wort **ein**.
Put the words **in the right order**.	**Bringe** die Wörter **in die richtige Reihenfolge.**
Put a circle around the right word • the letter in the chart.	Kreise das richtige Wort • den Buchstaben in der Tabelle ein.
Put the words in the right box.	Schreibe die Wörter in den richtigen Kasten.
Put the verbs in the simple past.	Setze die Verben in die einfache Vergangenheit.
Read the text.	**Lies** den Text.
Report what they say • what they said.	**Berichte**, was sie sagen • was sie gesagt haben.
Report the questions • the dialogue.	**Gib** die Fragen • den Dialog in indirekter Rede **wieder**.
Say it in a different way.	**Sage** es auf andere Weise.
Translate the sentences into German.	**Übersetze** die Sätze ins Deutsche.
Use the simple past • the present perfect.	**Benutze** die einfache Vergangenheit • das Perfekt.
What's that in English • in German?	Wie heißt das auf Englisch • auf Deutsch?
Write sentences • answers • questions • the dialogue • the interview …	**Schreibe** Sätze • Antworten • Fragen • den Dialog • das Interview …
Write about the picture/s.	Beschreibe das Bild/die Bilder.
Write the correct verb form.	Schreibe die richtige Form des Verbs.
Write questions to fit the answers.	Schreibe Fragen zu den Anworten.

List of irregular verbs

Hier findest du alle unregelmäßigen Verben, die im Buch vorkommen. Die Liste enthält jeweils alle drei Formen, auch wenn sie noch nicht alle in den Units vorgekommen sind.

infinitive	simple past	past participle	German
be [bi:]	was, were [wɒz, wɜ:]	been [bi:n]	sein
beat [bi:t]	beat [bi:t]	beaten ['bi:tn]	schlagen; besiegen
become [bɪ'kʌm]	became [bɪ'keɪm]	become [bɪ'kʌm]	werden
bleed [bli:d]	bled [bled]	bled [bled]	bluten
break [breɪk]	broke [brəʊk]	broken ['brəʊkn]	brechen
bring [brɪŋ]	brought [brɔ:t]	brought [brɔ:t]	bringen; mitbringen
build [bɪld]	built [bɪlt]	built [bɪlt]	bauen
burn [bɜ:n]	burned/burnt [bɜ:nt]	burned/burnt [bɜ:nt]	brennen
buy [baɪ]	bought [bɔ:t]	bought [bɔ:t]	kaufen
choose [tʃu:z]	chose [tʃəʊz]	chosen ['tʃəʊzn]	auswählen; wählen
come [kʌm]	came [keɪm]	come [kʌm]	kommen
cost [kɒst]	cost [kɒst]	cost [kɒst]	kosten
cut [kʌt]	cut [kʌt]	cut [kʌt]	(sich) schneiden
do [du:]	did [dɪd]	done [dʌn]	machen; tun
draw [drɔ:]	drew [dru:]	drawn [drɔ:n]	zeichnen
dream [dri:m]	dreamed/dreamt [dremt]	dreamed/dreamt [dremt]	träumen
drink [drɪŋk]	drank [dræŋk]	drunk [drʌŋk]	trinken
eat [i:t]	ate [eɪt]	eaten ['i:tn]	essen
fall [fɔ:l]	fell [fel]	fallen ['fɔ:ln]	fallen; hinfallen
feed [fi:d]	fed [fed]	fed [fed]	füttern; ernähren
feel [fi:l]	felt [felt]	felt [felt]	(sich) fühlen
fight [faɪt]	fought [fɔ:t]	fought [fɔ:t]	kämpfen; streiten
find [faɪnd]	found [faʊnd]	found [faʊnd]	finden
fly [flaɪ]	flew [flu:]	flown [fləʊn]	fliegen
forget [fə'get]	forgot [fə'gɒt]	forgotten [fə'gɒtn]	vergessen
freeze [fri:z]	froze [frəʊz]	frozen ['frəʊzn]	frieren; gefrieren
get [get]	got [gɒt]	got [gɒt]	bekommen; werden
give [gɪv]	gave [geɪv]	given ['gɪvn]	geben
go [gəʊ]	went [went]	gone [gɒn]	gehen; fahren
grow up [ˌgrəʊ_'ʌp]	grew up [ˌgru:_'ʌp]	grown up [ˌgrəʊn_'ʌp]	aufwachsen
hang [hæŋ]	hung [hʌŋ]	hung [hʌŋ]	hängen
have [hæv]	had [hæd]	had [hæd]	haben; besitzen
hear [hɪə]	heard [hɜ:d]	heard [hɜ:d]	hören
hide [haɪd]	hid [hɪd]	hidden ['hɪdn]	verstecken
hit [hɪt]	hit [hɪt]	hit [hɪt]	schlagen; treffen
hold [həʊld]	held [held]	held [held]	halten; festhalten
hurt [hɜ:t]	hurt [hɜ:t]	hurt [hɜ:t]	verletzen; weh tun
keep [ki:p]	kept [kept]	kept [kept]	halten
know [nəʊ]	knew [nju:]	known [nəʊn]	wissen; kennen
lay [leɪ]	laid [leɪd]	laid [leɪd]	legen; (den Tisch) decken
leave [li:v]	left [left]	left [left]	verlassen; lassen; abfahren

V

infinitive	simple past	past participle	German
lend [lend]	lent [lent]	lent [lent]	leihen; verleihen
lose [lu:z]	lost [lɒst]	lost [lɒst]	verlieren
make [meɪk]	made [meɪd]	made [meɪd]	machen; tun; bilden
mean [mi:n]	meant [ment]	meant [ment]	bedeuten; meinen
meet [mi:t]	met [met]	met [met]	kennen lernen; (sich) treffen
pay [peɪ]	paid [peɪd]	paid [peɪd]	bezahlen
put [pʊt]	put [pʊt]	put [pʊt]	setzen; legen; stellen
read [ri:d]	read [red]	read [red]	lesen
ride [raɪd]	rode [rəʊd]	ridden ['rɪdn]	fahren; reiten
ring [rɪŋ]	rang [ræŋ]	rung [rʌŋ]	klingeln; läuten
run [rʌn]	ran [ræn]	run [rʌn]	laufen; rennen
say [seɪ]	said [sed]	said [sed]	sagen; sprechen
see [si:]	saw [sɔ:]	seen [si:n]	sehen
sell [sel]	sold [səʊld]	sold [səʊld]	verkaufen
send [send]	sent [sent]	sent [sent]	schicken; senden
show [ʃəʊ]	showed [ʃəʊd]	shown [ʃəʊn]	zeigen
sing [sɪŋ]	sang [sæŋ]	sung [sʌŋ]	singen
sink [sɪŋk]	sank [sæŋk]	sunk [sʌŋk]	untergehen; sinken
sit [sɪt]	sat [sæt]	sat [sæt]	sitzen
sleep [sli:p]	slept [slept]	slept [slept]	schlafen
smell [smel]	smelled/smelt [smelt]	smelled/smelt [smelt]	riechen
speak [spi:k]	spoke [spəʊk]	spoken ['spəʊkn]	sprechen
spell [spel]	spelled/spelt [spelt]	spelled/spelt [spelt]	buchstabieren
spend [spend]	spent [spent]	spent [spent]	ausgeben; verbringen
stand [stænd]	stood [stʊd]	stood [stʊd]	stehen
sweep [swi:p]	swept [swept]	swept [swept]	fegen
swim [swɪm]	swam [swæm]	swum [swʌm]	schwimmen
take [teɪk]	took [tʊk]	taken ['teɪkn]	nehmen; mitnehmen
tell [tel]	told [təʊld]	told [təʊld]	erzählen; sagen
think [θɪŋk]	thought [θɔ:t]	thought [θɔ:t]	denken; glauben
throw [θrəʊ]	threw [θru:]	thrown [θrəʊn]	werfen
understand [ˌʌndə'stænd]	understood [ˌʌndə'stʊd]	understood [ˌʌndə'stʊd]	verstehen
wake up [weɪk‿'ʌp]	woke up [wəʊk‿'ʌp]	woken up [ˌwəʊkn‿'ʌp]	aufwachen
wear [weə]	wore [wɔ:]	worn [wɔ:n]	tragen
win [wɪn]	won [wʌn]	won [wʌn]	gewinnen; siegen
write [raɪt]	wrote [rəʊt]	written ['rɪtn]	schreiben